DB2 10 for z/OS
Cost Savings . . . Right Out of the Box

Dave Beulke

Roger Miller

Surekha Parekh

Julian Stuhler

MC PRESS

MC Press Online, LLC
Ketchum, ID 83340

DB2 10 for z/OS: Cost Savings . . . Right Out of the Box
Dave Beulke, Roger Miller, Surekha Parekh, and Julian Stuhler

First Edition
First Printing—September 2010

MC Press offers excellent discounts on this book when ordered in quantity for bulk purchases or special sales, which may include custom covers and content particular to your business, training goals, marketing focus, and branding interest.

MC Press Online, LLC
     Corporate Offices
     P.O. Box 4886
     Ketchum, ID 83340-4886 USA
For information regarding sales and/or customer service, please contact:
     MC Press
     P.O. Box 4300
     Big Sandy, TX 75755-4300 USA
For information regarding permissions or special orders, please contact:
     mcbooks@mcpressonline.com

ISBN: 978-158347-361-0

About the Authors

Dave Beulke (dave@davebeulke.com) is an internationally recognized DB2 consultant, author, and instructor known for his extensive expertise in database performance, data warehouses, and Internet applications. He is a member of the IBM DB2 Gold Consultant program, an IBM Information Champion, past president of the International DB2 Users Group (IDUG), co-author of the IBM DB2 V8 and V7 z/OS Administration and Business Intelligence Certification exams, columnist for *IBM Data Management Magazine*, and former instructor for The Data Warehouse Institute (TDWI). With more than 22 years of experience working with mainframe, UNIX®, and Windows® environments, Dave architects, redesigns, and tunes systems, databases, and applications, dramatically reducing CPU demand and saving his clients from CPU upgrades and millions in processing charges.

Roger Miller (millerrl@us.ibm.com) is a DB2 for z/OS technical evangelist, architect, and designer who has worked on many facets of DB2, ranging from overall design issues to SQL, languages, install, security, audit, standards, performance, concurrency, and availability. He is currently working to roll out DB2 10 and DB2 9 for z/OS and to design the next improvements in DB2. Roger has 31 years of experience on DB2 development, product design, and strategy. He helps customers use the product, answers many questions, and presents frequently to user groups. Roger holds a B.S. in Mathematics from Stanford University and an M.S. in Quantitative Methods of Business from UCLA.

Surekha Parekh (surekhaparekh@uk.ibm.com) is IBM's World-Wide Marketing Manager for DB2 for z/OS. She is responsible for market strategy, planning, and promotion of DB2 on System z®. Based in Warwick, United Kingdom, she is a passionate marketer with more than 25 years of business experience, and she is also passionate about DB2. Surekha represents IBM on the IDUG committee. IDUG is an independent DB2 user group with more than 16,000 members in more than 100 countries.

Julian Stuhler (julian.stuhler@triton.co.uk) is a Principal Consultant with Triton Consulting, a U.K.-based company specializing in the provision of DB2 consultancy, education, software, and managed services to clients throughout Europe. Julian has more than 20 years of relational database experience, working for clients in the insurance, telecommunications, banking, financial services, and manufacturing sectors. Julian has lectured widely on DB2 subjects, both in the United Kingdom and in Europe. He won the "Best Overall Speaker" award at the 2000 International DB2 User Group European Conference. Julian has co-authored an IBM Redbook on Java™ stored procedures and is a frequent contributor to industry publications such as *Database Journal*. He is an IBM DB2 Gold Consultant, past president of the Board of Directors for IDUG, and an IBM Data Champion.

Acknowledgements

The authors would like to thank the following people for their invaluable contributions to the content of this book:

- Maria Sueli Almeida, IBM® Silicon Valley Lab
- Rick Bowers, Director of DB2® for z/OS®
- John Campbell, Distinguished Engineer, DB2 for z/OS Development
- Ian Cook, DB2 for z/OS Product Introduction Manager
- Namik Hrle, Distinguished Engineer, IBM Boeblingen Laboratory
- Terrie Jacopi, DB2 for z/OS Program Manager
- Jeff Josten, Distinguished Engineer, DB2 for z/OS Development
- Philipp Nowak, BMW DB2 Product Manager
- Peter Paetsch, DB2 Consultant
- Mark Rader, IBM Advanced Technical Skills (ATS) Americas
- Paulo Sahadi, Senior Production Manager, Information Management Division, Banco do Brasil

Contents

DB2 10 for z/OS: CPU Savings . . . Right Out of the Box

Preface

We hope you enjoy our first book on DB2 10 for z/OS. DB2 10 is the most significant release we've shipped in more than a decade. We have focused our efforts around three clear themes: cost savings to our customers, simplifying database management with more automation, and providing proven technology.

The objective of this book is to give you not only an update on the latest functions, features, and benefits but also to provide you with valuable information from key members of the IBM DB2 for z/OS community whom you can contact. In addition, I wanted to ensure you are all aware of our virtual community, "The World of DB2 for z/OS" (*http://db2forzos.ning.com*), which is available 24x7 and currently has over 800 members. This one-stop shop hosts a collection of online resources, such as webcasts, white papers, blogs, virtual chats, videos, and more. Coupled with this virtual community there is also an independent DB2 user community (IDUG, *http://www.idug.org*) that hosts conferences in EMEA, North America, Australasia, and Asia Pacific each year. These communities are complimentary to all interested parties and are a great way to meet like-minded individuals, have fun, and at the same time grow and develop your DB2 skills. For a list of some additional sites dedicated to the DB2 for z/OS community, see the list at the end of this book.

The book is segmented in three sections:

- An introduction to DB2 10 by Roger Miller, highlighting the main features and functions and their associated business benefits, such as real CPU savings.
- A business value white paper by Julian Stuhler, independent DB2 consultant. Julian and I invited several beta clients to share not only their DB2 10 experiences but also perceived and actual business benefits.
- The last section of the book is another valuable paper written by Dave Beulke, who is also an independent consultant. This paper demonstrates how DB2 10 is a tremendous step forward in database technology because of its improvements in performance, scalability, availability, and security and application integration. Dave's paper focuses on performance enhancements.

I would like to thank Roger, Julian, and Dave for writing this book. Thank you, too, and enjoy the book. Do not hesitate to contact me directly.

Surekha Parekh
World-Wide Marketing Manager
IBM DB2 for z/OS
surekhaparekh@uk.ibm.com
September 2010

Why Read This Book?

Rick Bowers, Director of DB2 for z/OS

Why should customers read this book?
This book covers all the great features and functions that the team has worked so hard to provide in this release of DB2 10 for z/OS. The focus was on delivering business value and ensuring customers would be able to realize immediate benefit from the new release.

What new features/benefits will customers find in DB2 10 for z/OS?
Customers will find the release rich in performance and scalability enhancements. In addition, enhancements in important areas such as security, temporal support, and utilities round out this full-featured product.

About Rick Bowers
Rick (bowersrg@us.ibm.com) is the Director of DB2 for z/OS. He started in IBM as a developer and has managed both development and test organizations in STG and SWG. He has also managed key partner strategic alliances and business partner relationships in the Information Management group and was Director of the New Zealand software lab. In addition, he has been the Technical Account Executive at Wal-Mart and the Director of IBM's QSE Software Engineering Group.

John Campbell, IBM Distinguished Engineer

Why should customers read this book?
I strongly recommend reading this book to gain insight into the technical and business value of V10.

What new features/benefits will customers find in DB2 10 for z/OS?
1) The 64-bit SQL runtime provides significant virtual storage constraint relief, addressing the number one cause of DB2 crashes. Using more CICS®-DB2 protected **ENTRY** (persistent) threads and **RELEASE(DEALLOCATE)** provides the opportunity for significant price/performance improvement.

2) **INCLUDE** columns on unique indexes can reduce the number of indexes, enable faster insert and delete performance, and facilitate better SQL runtime performance through improved index filtering and/or index-only access. 3) Compression for SMF records can dramatically reduce the data volume at tiny additional CPU cost. 4) SQL pagination provides a new access method and targets performance improvements for existing SQL, including cursor-scrolling SQL and complex **OR** predicates against the same columns.

About John Campbell
John (campbelj@uk.ibm.com) is an IBM Distinguished Engineer reporting to the Director for z/OS Development at the IBM Silicon Valley Lab. He has extensive experience of DB2 in terms of systems, database, and applications design. John specializes in design for high performance and data sharing. He is one of IBM's foremost authorities for implementing high-end database/transaction-processing applications.

Surekha Parekh, World-Wide DB2 for z/OS Marketing Manager

Why should customers read this book?
This book helps explain the core benefits of DB2 for z/OS and enables customers and partners to quickly learn about the latest enhancements in DB2 10 and exploit this new technology to gain competitive edge.

What new features/benefits will customers find in DB2 10 for z/OS?
DB2 10 for z/OS provides exceptional CPU savings for most workloads, directly improving your bottom line and profitability. This benefit is timely under the current economic environment, in which companies are looking at reducing costs and getting more for less.

About Surekha Parekh
Surekha (surekhaparekh@uk.ibm.com) is IBM's World-Wide Marketing Manager for DB2 for z/OS. She is responsible for market strategy, planning, and promotion of DB2 on System z. Based in Warwick, United Kingdom, she is a passionate marketer with more than 25 years of business experience, and she is also passionate about DB2. Surekha represents IBM on the IDUG committee. IDUG is an independent DB2 user group with more than 16,000 members in more than 100 countries.

Roger Miller, DB2 for z/OS Technical Evangelist

Why should customers read this book?
This book provides a fast summary of DB2 10 and how to get there.

What new features/benefits will customers find in DB2 10 for z/OS?
DB2 10 for z/OS provides the best reduction in CPU for transactions and batch in 22 years. We expect most customers to reduce CPU times between 5 and 10 percent initially, with opportunity for more. Scalability is the second major benefit, with the ability to run five to 10 times as many threads in a single subsystem by moving 80 to 90 percent of the virtual storage above the bar. Schema evolution or data definition on demand enhancements improve availability. SQL and pureXML® improvements extend usability and application portability for this platform. Productivity improvements for application developers and for database administrators are also a key part of DB2 10.

About Roger Miller
Roger Miller (millerrl@us.ibm.com) is a DB2 for z/OS technical evangelist, architect, and designer who has worked on many facets of DB2. His jobs have ranged from overall design issues to SQL, languages, install, security, audit, standards, performance, concurrency, and availability in DB2 development, product design, and strategy over the past 31 years. Roger often helps customers to use the product, answers many questions, and presents frequently to user groups.

Namik Hrle, IBM Distinguished Engineer

Why should customers read this book?
This book provides a concise overview of the DB2 10 features and articulates well the key benefits customers can expect from migrating to the new DB2 release.

What new features/benefits will customers find in DB2 10 for z/OS?
DB2 10 addresses the key scalability challenges of modern workloads and is filled with features that benefit demanding enterprise applications. It is hard to single out any particular item because there are so many attractive features across the entire spectrum of database technology. I have great expectations in the area of overall performance and particularly from features that improve insert and query performance.

About Namik Hrle
Namik (hrle@de.ibm.com) is an IBM Distinguished Engineer in the IBM Boeblingen Laboratory. He is a member of the IBM Academy of Technology, Information Management Architecture Board, SWG Architecture Board Steering Committee, and many other IBM expert teams. Namik specializes in information management technology and its use by enterprise applications. He works closely with IBM labs worldwide and helps customers deploy and optimally exploit information management products.

Terrie Jacopi, DB2 for z/OS Program Manager

Why should customers read this book?
This book helps explain the core benefits of DB2 for z/OS, allowing you to get the most out of DB2 10.

What new features/benefits will customers find in DB2 10 for z/OS?
This release of DB2 provides unprecedented CPU savings for most workloads, making it easier to manage and even more cost-effective to run your business on DB2 for z/OS.

About Terrie Jacopi
Terrie (jacopi@us.ibm.com) is the DB2 for z/OS Program Manager at the IBM Silicon Valley Lab. She focuses on connecting the technical capabilities of DB2 and System z with the business value delivered.

Introduction

by Roger Miller

Customers need to reduce costs and adapt quickly to support business growth, without sacrificing the resiliency required for today's demanding business requirements. Version 10 of IBM® DB2® for z/OS® (DB2 10) addresses those needs, building on the capabilities of DB2 9 for z/OS and the System z® platform.

DB2 10 for z/OS delivers innovations in the following key areas.

- ***Reduced DB2 CPU time for out-of-the-box savings.*** DB2 10 delivers great value by reducing CPU usage. Most customers can achieve out-of-the-box CPU savings of 5 to 10 percent for traditional workloads and up to 20 percent for some workloads. Improved scalability and constraint relief can add to the savings.

- ***Unsurpassed resiliency for business-critical information.*** DB2 10 innovations raise the bar on data resiliency through scalability improvements, fewer outages, and improved security. DB2 10 delivers the ability to handle up to five to 10 times more active concurrent users in a single DB2 subsystem. Customers can scale up or scale out simply, and with less system management. Schema evolution lets you make more changes while business keeps running.

- ***Rapid application and warehouse deployment for business growth.*** SQL and pureXML® enhancements in DB2 10 help productivity, improve performance, and simplify application ports to DB2 for z/OS. DB2 10 adds unique capabilities to support temporal data using business and system time within the database itself, making application development and maintenance simpler and more reliable.

Now let's provide a little more detail to explain the improvements.

Improved Performance and Reduced CPU for Out-of-the-Box Savings

DB2 10 delivers by improving performance and reducing CPU usage. Most customers can achieve out-of-the-box CPU savings of 5 to 10 percent for traditional workloads and up to 20 percent for specific workloads described below. Measurements compare to previous releases of DB2 for z/OS. **REBIND** is needed to obtain the best performance and memory improvements. DB2 reduces CPU usage by optimizing processor times and memory access, leveraging the latest processor improvements, larger amounts of memory, and z/OS enhancements. Improved scalability and constraint relief can add to the savings. Productivity improvements for database and systems administrators can drive even more savings.

In DB2 10, performance improvements focus on reducing CPU processing time without causing significant administration or application changes. Most performance improvements are implemented by simply migrating to DB2 10 and rebinding.

You gain significant performance improvements from distributed data facility (DDF) optimization, buffer pool enhancements, parallelism enhancements, and more.

Early DB2 10 performance benchmarking and customer experience has shown a 5 to 10 percent CPU reduction in transactions after rebinding. Some customers may get more or some less CPU reduction depending on the workload. Customers who have scalability issues, such as virtual storage constraints or latching, can see higher improvements. Opportunities for tuning can take advantage of memory improvements. High-volume, short-running distributed transactions can take advantage of CPU reductions, using **RELEASE(DEALLOCATE)**.

Concurrent sequential insert CPU time can be reduced from 5 to 40 percent. Queries can be improved as much as 20 percent without access path change, and more for better access paths. A native SQL procedure workload has shown up to 20 percent CPU reduction using **SET** statements, **IF** statements, and **SYSDUMMY1**. Customers moving from DB2 9 should expect a small (0 to 7 percent) reduction in CPU times for utilities, while customers moving from DB2 V8 will see larger CPU reductions in the range of 20 percent.

Productivity Improvements

New SQL and XML capabilities improve productivity for those who develop new applications and for those who are porting applications from other platforms. Automating, reducing, or eliminating tasks and avoiding manual actions improves productivity and can help avoid problems. Resiliency improvements for virtual storage and availability increase productivity. DB2 10 improvements make the install, migration, and service processes faster and more reliable. Installation and migration information has been improved, using customer feedback.

Flexibility in Migration Paths

For this release, you can upgrade to DB2 10 directly from a DB2 Version 8 subsystem in new function mode (NFM) without starting the system in DB2 9. This provides customers greater flexibility to meet their business needs and to save time getting to DB2 10. Several process improvements make the upgrade simpler.

Unsurpassed Resiliency for Business-Critical Information

Business resiliency is a key component of the value proposition of DB2 for z/OS, System z hardware, the z/OS operating system, and other key System z software, such as IMS™ and CICS®. Resiliency helps to keep your business running even during unexpected circumstances. Innovations in DB2 10 drive new value in resiliency through scalability improvements and fewer outages, whether those outages are planned or unplanned. Virtual storage enhancements deliver the ability to handle five to 10 times more concurrent active users in a single DB2 subsystem than in previous releases of DB2 (as many as 20,000 concurrent active threads). Improved availability is supported by allowing more changes using schema evolution or data definition on demand. Security improvements also contribute to robust business resiliency.

Continuous Availability Enhancements

DB2 10 provides online schema enhancements that allow you to make changes to database objects (indexes and table spaces) while maximizing the availability of the altered objects. Through enhancements to **ALTER** statements, you can now change more attributes of indexes and table spaces without having to unload the data, drop and re-create the objects, regenerate all the security authorizations, re-create the views, and reload the data. The changes are materialized when the altered objects are reorganized. DB2 10 allows fast changes of table space types, page sizes, data set sizes, and segment sizes. Conversion to universal table spaces is much simpler.

In addition, DB2 10 improves the usability and performance of online reorganization in several key ways. It supports the reorganization of disjoint partition ranges of a partitioned table space (also in DB2 9 now) and improves **SWITCH** phase performance and diagnostics. Also, DB2 10 removes restrictions related to online reorganization of base table spaces that use LOB columns.

Reduced Catalog Contention

In DB2 10, the DB2 catalog is restructured to reduce lock contention by removing all links in the catalog and directory. In addition, new functionality improves the lock avoidance techniques of DB2 and improves concurrency by holding acquired locks for less time and preventing writers from blocking the readers of data.

In DB2 10 NFM, you can access currently committed data to minimize transaction suspension. Now, a read transaction can access the currently committed and consistent image of rows that are incompatibly locked by write transactions without being blocked. Using this type of concurrency control can greatly reduce timeout situations between readers and writers who are accessing the same data row.

Virtual Storage Relief

Enhancements in DB2 10 substantially increase the capacity of a single DB2 subsystem by removing virtual storage and other constraints. This release moves most memory to 64-bit, which provides virtual storage relief and can greatly improve the vertical scalability of your DB2 subsystem while minimizing administration. In addition, a 64-bit ODBC driver is now available on DB2 9 and 10.

Security Enhancements

This release of DB2 provides critical enhancements to security and auditing, strengthening DB2 security in the z/OS environment. For example, DB2 10 provides increased granularity for DB2 administrative authority and offers a new DB2 data security solution that enables you to manage access to a table at the level of a row, a column, or both. In addition, you can define and create different audit policies to address the various security needs of your business.

Rapid Application and Warehouse Deployment for Business Growth

SQL, pureXML®, and optimization enhancements in DB2 10 help extend usability, improve performance, and ease application portability to DB2. DB2 10 delivers significant query improvements, with better performance and CPU reductions, allowing you to manage and maintain your data in a single platform infrastructure with single audit and security processes, and, most important, providing a single answer based on your core operational data.

SQL Improvements

SQL enhancements deliver new function for improved productivity and DB2 family consistency and simplify application porting to DB2 for z/OS from other platforms and database management systems. Enhancements are provided for SQL scalar functions, and SQL table functions are added. Native SQL procedure language (SQL PL) is easier and faster. Implicit casting makes porting simpler, as DB2 SQL is more consistent with other products and platforms. Allowing more flexibility in the number of digits for fractions of seconds and allowing timestamps with time zones simplifies porting. Moving sums and moving averages help in warehouse queries and in porting.

Temporal Tables and Versioning

In this release of DB2 for z/OS, you have a lot of flexibility in how you can query data based on periods of time. DB2 supports two types of periods, the system time (**SYSTEM_TIME**) period and the business time (**BUSINESS_TIME**) period. The **SYSTEM_TIME** period is a system-maintained period in which DB2 maintains the beginning and ending timestamp values for a row. For the **BUSINESS_TIME** period, you maintain the beginning and ending values for a row. Support of business time and system time allows for significant simplification of applications, pushing the complicated handling of these concepts down to the database engine itself.

In addition, DB2 10 introduces versioning, which is the process of keeping historical versions of rows for a temporal table that is defined with a **SYSTEM_TIME** period, or both time periods, allowing for simple retrieval of key historical data.

pureXML Improvements

DB2 10 improves DB2 family consistency and productivity for pureXML users. These improvements also deliver excellent performance improvements. DB2 10 delivers binary XML format, XML schema validation as a built-in function, XML date and time data types and functions, XML parameters in routines, and much more.

Enhanced Business Analytics and Math Functions with QMF

Query Management Facility (QMF™) Version 10 has new analytic and math-ematical functions and OLAP support. Providing access to many more data sources via JDBC opens QMF to a wider array of information that can be combined with DB2 within the same report.

DB2 10 for z/OS:
A Smarter Database
for a Smarter Planet™

by Julian Stuhler

Executive Summary

DB2 10 for z/OS is the latest release of IBM's flagship database. The following sections provide a high-level overview of the major new features from an IT executive's perspective, with the emphasis on the underlying business value that DB2 10 can deliver.

DB2 10 delivers a number of significant business benefits, many of which are exploitable "out of the box" with little or no database, application, or system changes. These can be summarized as follows:

- *CPU reductions.* DB2 includes a raft of enhancements aimed at improving application performance and reducing CPU usage. Most customers can expect to see net CPU savings of 5 to 10 percent in their traditional DB2 workload compared with DB2 9, without any application changes being required. Significant additional savings are possible for other specific workloads, and with some application changes.

- *Scalability improvements.* DB2 10 delivers a spectacular increase in the number of threads that can be supported by a single subsystem—most customers will be able to achieve 5 to 10 times the number of concurrent connections compared with DB2 9. This will allow many customers to reduce the number of DB2 members needed to support their workloads, resulting in net CPU and memory savings and improving application performance.

- *Productivity enhancements.* New features such as temporal tables, automated statistics, and improved dynamic schema change reduce the effort required by developers and support staff to deliver robust DB2 applications.

Even in the most favorable economic climate, businesses need to control costs and increase efficiency in order to improve their bottom line. In today's more challenging business environment, this has become a key factor for the survival and success of enterprises of all sizes.

DB2 10 delivers significant "out of the box" benefits that many customers will be able to exploit with little or no additional effort. These include the most aggressive performance and CPU improvements of any DB2 release in the past 20 years, scalability enhancements to support ever-increasing workloads, and productivity improvements to allow DB2 developers and support staff to respond more rapidly to the demands of the business.

Collectively, these features deliver real and quantifiable business benefit, and many customers will be considering upgrading to DB2 10 much more quickly than they may have done for previous releases.

"Continuous availability, reduced performance cost, and future growth with constraints are of paramount importance to our business. We are really excited about the potential of DB2 10 for z/OS to help us achieve our goals in each of these areas. Our high expectation is the reason why Danske Bank will invest a lot of effort in the Beta program."

— Jan Michael Christensen, Vice President, Danske Bank

Section I

Introduction

You don't have to be an IT professional to see that the world around us is getting smarter. Everywhere you look, our environment is getting more connected and "instrumented," and clever technologies are being adopted to use the resulting real-time data to make things safer, quicker, and greener. While this explosion in machine-generated data is happening, human beings themselves are also generating vastly more content than ever before. Today, people and machines together create new data at an astounding rate: more data will be created over the next four years than in the entire history of the planet.

Building a smarter planet is going to need smarter IT systems, which in turn will depend upon the availability of a robust, efficient, and secure way of storing, retrieving and analyzing this vast amount of data. From banking to transportation to healthcare, DB2 for z/OS sits at the heart of many of the IT systems needed to drive a Smarter Planet[1] and has an important role to play in supporting the transformation.

In the meantime, the global economic climate remains challenging, and DB2 for z/OS customers around the world are still trying to gain competitive advantage by doing more with less: more business insight, more performance, more operational efficiency, more functionality, more productivity with less cost, quicker time to market, and a lower total cost of ownership (TCO).

DB2 10 for z/OS, the latest release of IBM's flagship database, seeks to address these and other challenges. A wealth of material exists on the technical changes within DB2 10, but finding descriptions of how those new features will improve your business results can be a challenge. This paper provide a high-level overview of the major new features from an IT executive's perspective, with the emphasis on the underlying business value that DB2 10 can deliver.

In the meantime, many customers are still running DB2 for z/OS Version 8 (or earlier releases) and need to understand how DB2 9 can help their organization. A brief summary of the business benefits offered by DB2 9 is provided in the Appendix (page 59).

Section II

DB2 10: A Smarter Database

In this section, we take a detailed look at the major features of DB2 10 and the ways many of IBM's most innovative enterprise customers are intending to use them to deliver an enhanced IT service to the business.

Many of these enhancements can be used "out of the box" with little or no effort required to begin exploiting them, reducing the time to value for a DB2 10 upgrade.

This section is organized around the key DB2 10 themes:

- Efficiency: Reducing cost and improving productivity
- Resilience: Improving availability and data security
- Growth: Supporting new and expanding workloads
- Business Analytics: Enhanced query and reporting

Efficiency

Even in the most favorable economic climate, businesses need to control costs and increase efficiency to improve their bottom line. In today's more challenging business environment, this has become a key factor for the survival and success of enterprises of all sizes.

This section examines the major DB2 10 enhancements aimed at improving the efficiency of the IT systems that rely on DB2: a key design objective for the new release. These features can help to reduce ongoing operational costs, improve developer and DBA productivity, and enhance the customer's experience by increasing performance and delivering a more responsive application.

CPU Reductions

Most DB2 for z/OS customers operate on a CPU usage-based charging model, so increases or decreases in the amount of CPU required to run DB2 applications can have a direct and significant impact on overall operational costs. Traditionally, IBM has tried to limit the additional CPU cost of adding new functionality into each release, keeping the net CPU impact below 5 percent.

The move to a 64-bit computing platform in DB2 V8 was an exception to this rule, and it introduced some significant processing overheads that resulted in many customers experiencing net CPU increases of 5 to 10 percent following the upgrade. DB2 9[2] helped to redress the balance somewhat by delivering modest CPU improvements for many large customers, but IBM was determined to deliver more significant cost reductions in DB2 10.

One of the fundamental design objectives of DB2 10 was to deliver a 5 to 10 percent CPU reduction "out of the box," with little or no change being required to applications and further savings being possible with some database and/or application changes. Figure 1 shows a pictorial representation of the typical CPU decrease seen in each release since V3.

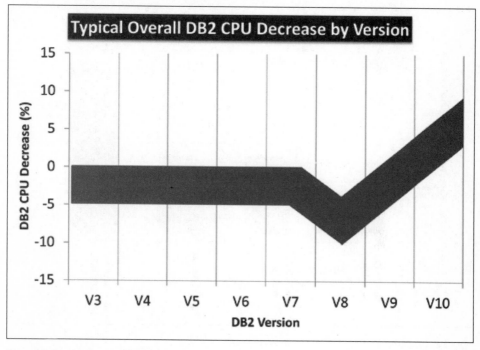

Figure 1: Typical overall CPU decrease by version

Based on IBM labs tests and some early beta customer experiences, IBM has exceeded this objective and delivered the most aggressive performance and CPU improvements of any DB2 release in the past 20 years. As many of these improvements are down to internal DB2 code optimization and exploitation of the latest System z hardware instructions, most customers can expect to see CPU savings of 5 to 10 percent in their traditional DB2 workload without any application changes[3] being required.

Figure 2 shows the savings relative to DB2 9 that were achieved in internal IBM testing using the standard IBM Relational Warehouse Workload (IRWW). The first column shows a 3.7 percent CPU saving immediately following migration in DB2 10 compatibility mode (CM). The net saving increased to 7.4 percent following a **REBIND** of the affected packages with the same access path, and this remained the same when the system was placed in new function mode (NFM). Finally, a net saving of 17.4 percent was measured once the packages had been rebound to use the new **RELEASE** protocols described elsewhere in this document.

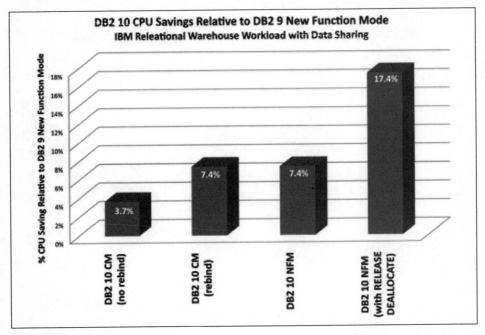

Figure 2: Sample CPU savings using IRWW

Customers running the following types of workload can expect even bigger CPU savings:

- Workloads previously constrained due to a lack of virtual storage in DB2 V8 or 9.
- Distributed applications connecting to DB2 via the DRDA protocol (e.g., SAP).

- Workloads using native SQL stored procedures. Efficiency enhancements with commonly used functions[4] have shown CPU reductions of up to 20 percent during initial IBM labs testing.
- Workloads with heavy concurrent insert activity, especially where rows are inserted sequentially, where savings of 5 to 40 percent have been observed in the labs.
- Complex query workloads, where up to 20 percent CPU reduction has been observed with no change to the access path. Greater savings are possible where a more efficient access path is selected.

All of these figures assume an upgrade from DB2 9 to DB2 10. For those customers considering a move directly from DB2 V8 to DB2 10,[5] the net impact could be even bigger.

Most of the performance measurements available at the time of writing are based on internal IBM lab workloads, but early indications from beta customers show CPU savings in line with the lab tests. The potential CPU savings made possible by DB2 10 are likely to be the single biggest factor in driving customers to upgrade to the new release—especially as many of the savings can be realized very quickly after the upgrade, and with few or no application changes.

Temporal Tables

Many IT systems need to keep some form of historical information in addition to the current status for a given business object. For example, a financial institution may need to retain the previous addresses of a customer, as well as the current one, and may need to know which address applied at any given time. Equally, an insurance company may need to know what level of coverage was in place two months ago when a claim was made. Previously, these kinds of requirements would have required the DBA and application developers to spend valuable time creating and testing the code, as well as associated database design to support the historical perspective while minimizing any performance impact.

The new temporal data support in DB2 10 provides this functionality as part of the core database engine. The DBA indicates which tables/columns require temporal support when they are created, and DB2 maintains the history automatically whenever an update is made to the data. Elegant SQL support lets the developer query the database with an "as of" date, which will return the information that was current at the specified time.

As shown in Figure 3, DB2 maintains a separate "history table" for updated rows in a temporal table. This is completely transparent to the developer, who codes SQL against the main table as usual. When a row is updated (as shown at time T3 in the diagram), DB2 will store a version of the old row in the history table before updating the current row in the main table. Similarly, when a row is deleted, it is first copied to the history table before being removed from the main table. DB2 maintains system timestamps (the **SYS_START** and **SYS_END** columns shown) to record the period during which a given version of the row was current.

Finally, the new **AS OF** clause in SQL **SELECT** statements lets the developer see the data as it was at a given point of time. In the example, the policy information at time T2 is required, which will return the original address (**A3**) instead of the current address (**A4**).

With so many IT systems needing to accommodate a historical perspective and maintain audit logs of changes made to sensitive data, DB2's new temporal

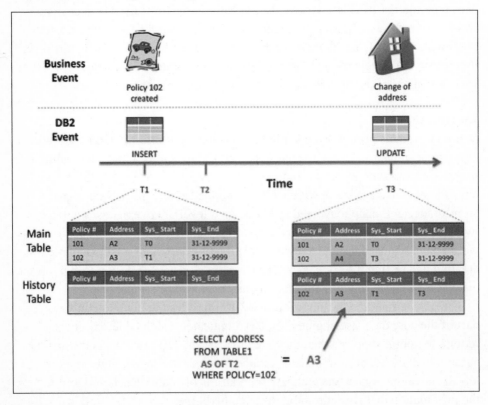

Figure 3: DB2 temporal data concepts

support promises to save many hundreds of hours of design, coding, and testing that would otherwise be required to build this function manually for each application. While the benefit for existing applications is limited, this feature promises to deliver major productivity savings for new developments.

Improved Scalability

The valuable scalability enhancements within DB2 10 are described elsewhere in this document. In addition to supporting workload growth and providing more flexibility, these enhancements can deliver some significant performance benefits, as follows:

Reduction in data sharing overhead. The virtual storage constraints within previous releases of DB2 imposed a practical limit of 400 to 500 concurrent active threads[6] within a single DB2 subsystem. As a result, many DB2 data sharing[7] customers were forced to use more DB2 members than otherwise necessary to support their workloads. Although DB2's industry-leading data sharing architecture minimizes the processing overheads, each additional member will impact overall performance and resource usage.

Figure 4 shows a typical scenario for an SAP environment. In this example, a data sharing group consisting of four DB2 members is used to support 1,600 concurrent threads from four SAP application servers.

DB2 10 introduces some dramatic scalability improvements that allow each system to handle five to 10 times the current number threads. This will allow

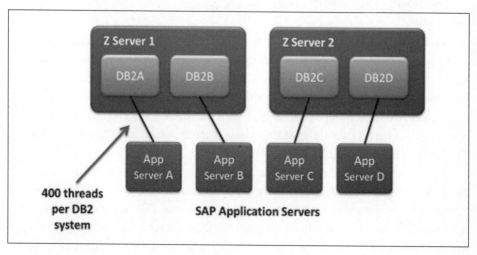

Figure 4: Typical SAP data sharing configuration

many customers to reduce the number of DB2 members needed to support their workloads, resulting in net CPU and memory savings and improving application performance.

This benefit is illustrated by Figure 5, which shows that the same 1,600-thread workload can be handled by just two DB2 subsystems, with significant scope for additional workload growth. (Initial SAP benchmarks show 2,500 threads per DB2 system is sustainable.) Productivity savings are also possible due to the reduced requirement to closely monitor available storage.

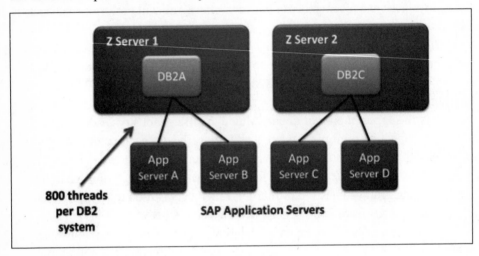

Figure 5: Potential DB2 10 SAP data sharing configuration

Improved dynamic statement caching. With the growing popularity of running Java™ and ERP workloads such as SAP on DB2 for z/OS, dynamic SQL[8] is becoming more and more prevalent. DB2 allows dynamic SQL statements to be cached in order to avoid most of the overheads usually associated with executing dynamic SQL, but the size of this cache was limited in previous releases due to the same virtual storage constraints described above. This in turn limited the effectiveness of the cache.

The virtual storage constraint relief delivered in DB2 10 will enable most customers to dramatically increase the size of the dynamic statement cache, thereby allowing a greater proportion of their dynamic SQL to be cached and reducing CPU and elapsed times for these queries. Other important enhancements that will improve dynamic statement caching in DB2 10 are described elsewhere in this document.

Together, these scalability enhancements give DB2 customers more flexibility in the way they distribute their workload across the available System z servers, while reducing DB2 CPU usage and improving the performance of key application processes.

New Hash Access Method

Many high-volume OLTP applications need to efficiently access a single row via a fully qualified primary key, but most of the access paths available to DB2 today are optimized for accessing sets of rows. Previously, the most efficient access path for a single-row fetch would have been via a unique index on the table, as shown in Figure 6.

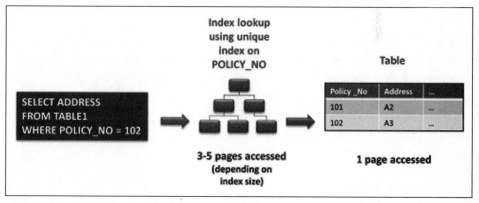

Figure 6: Single-row access via unique index

While this access path can be highly efficient if multiple rows need to be accessed sequentially, the overhead of navigating the index structure can be expensive for single-row access. Depending on the size of the data, the preceding example would typically require DB2 to access a total of 4 to 6 pages in the index and table, some of which might also require a physical I/O operation to pull the page into the buffer pool if it isn't already resident.

DB2 10 introduces a completely new access method, known as Hash Access. Where a table has been enabled for Hash Access, the vast majority of requests for a single row using the unique key will be satisfied with a single page access[9] because DB2 will use the key as input to a hashing algorithm that will produce the page number and row offset needed to directly access the given row (Figure 7).

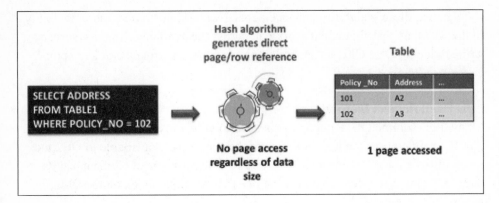

Figure 7: Single-row access via a hash

Hash access tables are not without their disadvantages: they will require 20 to 100 percent more disk space than traditional types and could be more expensive to access for multiple-row access. However, for many high-performance applications that predominantly use single-row access, these limitations could be an acceptable tradeoff for significantly reduced CPU (due to fewer pages accessed) and potentially lower I/O and elapsed times (if physical I/O operations are avoided for index page access).

Automated Statistics

One of the most important factors in DB2 query performance is the access path chosen by DB2, and that is heavily influenced by the table and index statistics gathered by the **RUNSTATS** utility. The old adage of "garbage in, garbage out" is very relevant to access path selection, so an important part of any DBA's job is to ensure that accurate, up-to-date statistics are available for critical tables.

RUNSTATS can be scheduled to run at fixed times, but this doesn't allow for ad hoc processes that can significantly change the table characteristics. A simple scheduled approach can result in statistics not being gathered often enough (leading to poor access paths and increased CPU/elapsed time) or too often (wasting the CPU used by the **RUNSTATS** utility).

A new automated statistics feature enables DB2 10 to dynamically monitor the currency of table and index statistics and automatically schedule the necessary **RUNSTATS** job when required. This frees the DBA to focus on more demanding activities, improving productivity and potentially reducing CPU requirements due to improved access paths and/or elimination of unnecessary **RUNSTATS** jobs.

Include Additional Columns in Unique Index

When a primary key is formally defined on a table, DB2 requires a unique index to be defined. In previous versions of DB2, that index could contain only the primary key columns. If additional columns were required to support specific SQL statements (such as the **SELECT** statement shown in Figure 8), it was necessary to create a separate additional index.

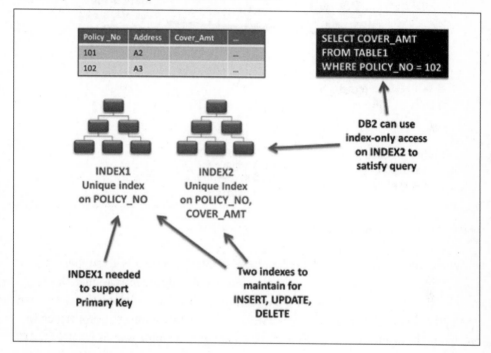

Figure 8: Multiple indexes to support index-only access

This approach allowed the SQL statement to be executed efficiently but added unnecessary overheads to **INSERT**, **UPDATE**, and **DELETE** operations as two indexes needed to be maintained rather than one.

DB2 10 allows columns other than the unique key to be specified in the index definition. As shown in Figure 9, this allows the second index to be dropped, removing the DASD, CPU, and I/O overheads associated with that index while continuing to support the efficient access path needed by the **SELECT** statement.

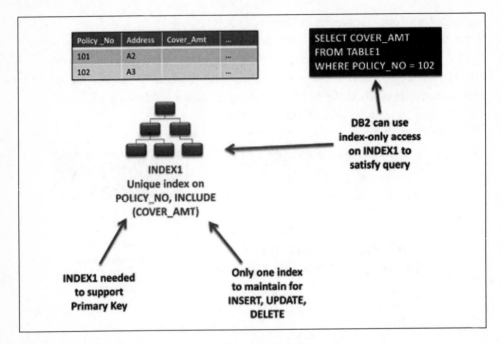

Figure 9: Single index with non-unique columns included

Where additional indexes have had to be created specifically to support this kind of access, removal of the redundant index will significantly reduce the cost of any update operations against the underlying table. Initial lab tests have shown up to 30 percent CPU reduction in **INSERT**, with identical query performance in one example where two indexes were replaced with a single one using **INCLUDE** columns.

Buffer Pool Enhancements

As processor speeds continue to increase at a faster rate than disk subsystems, the relative cost of performing random I/O operations is increasing, and minimizing I/O has become a major objective in improving performance. DB2's buffer pools cache frequently accessed data in memory, avoiding physical I/O activity and significantly improving performance.

DB2 10 introduces a number of new enhancements for buffer pools that should yield significant performance benefits.

Large page support. With the move to a 64-bit computing platform in DB2 V8, it became possible to define dramatically bigger buffer pools (up to 1TB). However, the size of each hardware "page" within the pool remained at 4KB (Figure 10), so large pools can have many millions of pages, leading to increased z/OS overheads.

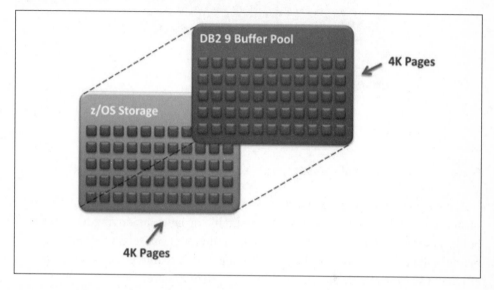

Figure 10: Buffer pool using 4KB z/OS page size

IBM's z10 and newer z196 servers are able to support 1MB page sizes within the hardware (Figure 11), which will result in fewer pages and more efficient access to data within the DB2 buffer pools. Internal IBM testing has shown CPU reductions of 1 to 4 percent with this feature enabled.

In-memory pagesets. Many DB2 applications make extensive use of "code tables": small, frequently referenced lookup tables. Such tables are often performance-critical and are placed in separate buffer pools that have been sized to ensure that all data remains in storage to avoid any I/O delays. A new attribute introduced in DB2 10 allows a given buffer pool to be marked as "in memory." DB2 will automatically read all data into this buffer pool at startup (avoiding I/O delays the first time a given data page is accessed), and the optimizer will assume a zero I/O cost when assessing the cost of accessing the table. This enhancement could further improve access times to these performance-critical tables.

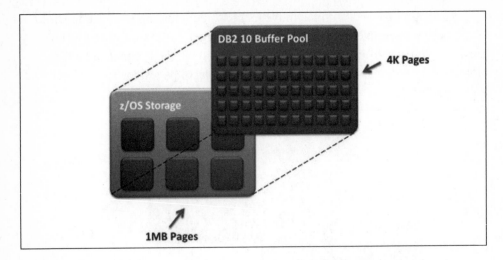

Figure 11: Buffer pool using 1MB z/OS page size

Memory allocation on demand. In previous versions of DB2, the full amount of storage was allocated as soon as the first table or index belonging to a given buffer pool was allocated. Oversized pools could therefore reserve storage that was never used. DB2 10 allocates storage as it is required, allowing more efficient use of available storage within the System z server.

Dynamic Statement Cache Enhancements

As mentioned elsewhere in this document, dynamic SQL is becoming more and more prevalent, and DB2 allows dynamic SQL statements to be cached to avoid most of the overheads usually associated with executing SQL in this way. However, the dynamic statement cache previously relied on SQL statements being identical to be able to re-use the cached statement.

In the example shown in Figure 12, the two SQL statements are different (they are selecting a different policy number), and therefore they will be separately cached even though the access path taken is likely to be identical for each one. This uses up valuable space in the dynamic statement cache and forces DB2 to fully re-prepare each statement, causing significant CPU and performance overheads for high-volume transactions.

Although it is possible to address this issue in previous releases through the use of parameter markers,[10] many dynamic SQL applications do not use them due to the effort involved in changing the code. Each SQL statement and the surrounding code must be changed, which could add up to many hundreds of lines of code for some applications.

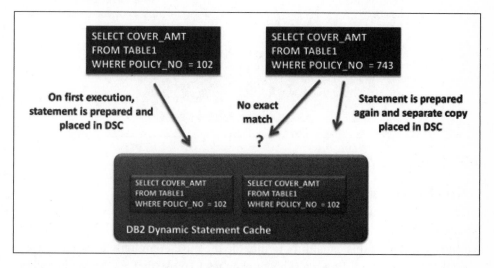

Figure 12: DSC with no parameter markers – previous releases

DB2 10 delivers an important enhancement that lets DB2 recognize that an incoming dynamic SQL statement is fundamentally the same as a previously cached version, even when parameter markers have not been coded by the developer, as shown in Figure 13.

To enable this feature, a single statement property has to be set within the code. Although this still requires the application code to be changed, the scope and magnitude of the change is much less than that required to implement parameter markers.

This feature will significantly decrease the effort required to enable dynamic SQL statement re-use, which in turn could increase the proportion of dynamic SQL applications able to benefit from the dynamic statement cache, driving down CPU costs and allowing better use to be made of the storage devoted to the cache.

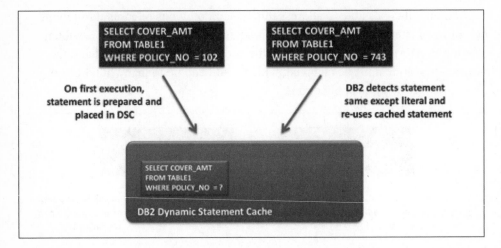

Figure 13: DSC with no parameter markers – DB2 10

Enhanced Dynamic Schema Change

DB2 V8 introduced some major enhancements to allow database structures to be altered dynamically; this capability was further enhanced in DB2 9. IBM continues to extend this capability to include the most commonly used changes, and DB2 10 adds the following schema changes to those that can be made online:

- Altering the table space type, to allow older table spaces to be converted to the newer "universal table space" format introduced in DB2 9.[11] Universal table spaces can greatly simplify space management, improving both DBA productivity and data availability.
- Altering the **MEMBER CLUSTER** attribute. This is an important performance optimization in a data sharing environment and requires significant DBA effort and data outage to implement prior to DB2 10.
- Altering table space page size, dataset size, segment size, and index page size. These parameters can have a significant impact on I/O performance, and DB2 9 introduced some new options that this enhancement will make easier and quicker to implement.

Dynamic schema change significantly improves data availability, but it also reduces the possibility of human error and improves DBA productivity because complex scripts to drop and re-create database objects can be replaced by a single SQL statement.

Optimizer Enhancements

DB2 10 includes a number of enhancements to DB2's industry-leading optimizer—the key component that allows DB2 to pick the most efficient access path for a given query. These include:

Safe query optimization. The DB2 optimizer often has to make educated guesses about the amount of data that will be filtered by a given predicate in an SQL statement. Enhancements to the optimizer in DB2 10 enable it to take into account the degree of confidence it has with these estimates, letting it choose a slightly more expensive access path if it has significantly lower risk associated with it.

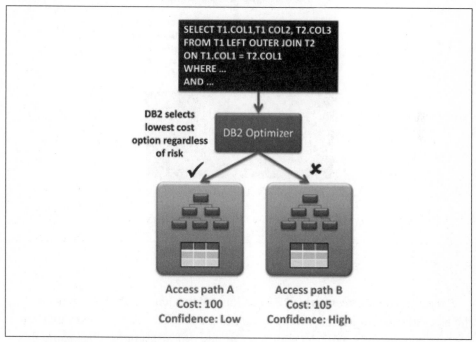

Figure 14: Optimization based on cost

In the example shown in Figure 14, a previous version of DB2 will select the access path with the lowest estimated cost, regardless of the degree of uncertainty associated with any filtering predicates.

In a second example, shown in Figure 15, the DB2 10 optimizer takes into account the facts that access path B has only a marginally higher estimated cost but the degree of confidence in the estimate is much higher, and it selects this access path instead.

This feature increases the consistency of the access path decisions made by DB2, enabling more predictable performance across the many different environments it has to support in today's enterprise.

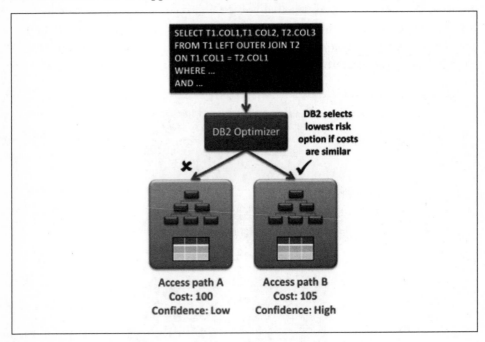

Figure 15: Safe optimization

Parallelism enhancements. DB2 has long supported the ability to reduce the elapsed time for key processes by splitting them into multiple tasks that can execute concurrently. DB2 10 removes a number of restrictions when using this CPU parallelism, allowing it to be used in more situations than previous editions.

As much as 80 percent of the CPU time for large parallel SQL queries can be redirected to zIIP processors,[12] so this also has the potential to reduce overall CPU costs for the DB2 workload.

Improved predicate filtering. When DB2 executes a query, two stages of processing can be involved. Stage 1 processing is responsible for retrieving the data pages from the buffer and initial filtering by applying simpler predicates. If necessary, Stage 2 processing then applies any remaining predicates before the data is passed back to the application, as shown in Figure 16.

Predicates applied during Stage 1 processing are more efficient because they allow more data to be filtered earlier in the process. DB2 10 includes an enhancement that allows some predicates (such as scalar functions) to be evaluated at Stage 1 rather than Stage 2, as was previously the case. This can significantly decrease the overall cost of a query, reducing the amount of CPU and elapsed time necessary to execute it.

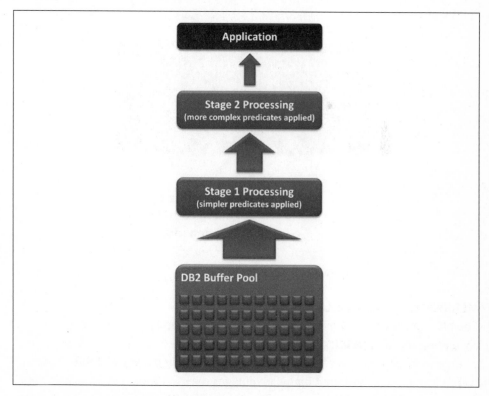

Figure 16: Stage 1 and Stage 2 query processing

Improved index access. DB2 10 includes several enhancements to improve index access. A new access path allows DB2 to scan an index just once where several **OR** predicates can all use the same index, whereas previous versions would have scanned the index multiple times. A technique known as "predicate transitive closure" lets DB2 use predicates supplied by the user in a query to derive additional predicates and potentially improve the access path chosen. DB2 has been able to use this technique for some time, but DB2 10 is now able to also apply it to **IN**-list queries, as shown in the example in Figure 17.

Together, these optimizer enhancements further consolidate DB2's position as having the most sophisticated and effective optimizer in the industry, able to minimize overall CPU demand through the selection of the most efficient access path. Although several of these enhancements will require DB2 packages to be rebound, another enhancement known as Plan Stability (described elsewhere in this document) removes the main inhibitor to such enhancements being fully exploited.

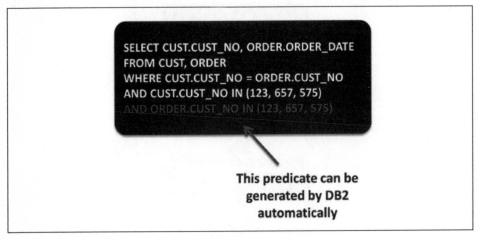

Figure 17: Predicate transitive closure for in-lists

MEMBER CLUSTER for Universal Table Spaces

The **MEMBER CLUSTER** table space option can dramatically reduce lock contention for high **INSERT** activity in a data sharing environment and is a commonly used tuning tool. DB2 9 introduced the new Universal Table Space (UTS) format, which offered many advantages over traditional table spaces[13] but did not support the **MEMBER CLUSTER** option. The DBA therefore had to choose between implementing **MEMBER CLUSTER** (which required a change to non-UTS table spaces and a drop and re-create of the table) or staying with UTS and living without the benefits of **MEMBER CLUSTER**. This was a particular problem in SAP environments, as recent versions of SAP make extensive use of UTS table spaces.

DB2 10 removes this restriction and allows **MEMBER CLUSTER** to be specified for UTS table spaces. As previously discussed, the DB2 10 enhancements to dynamic schema change also enable **MEMBER CLUSTER** to be implemented via a simple **ALTER** rather than requiring the table space to be dropped and re-created. These changes give the DBA more flexibility in improving application performance within a data sharing environment, with greatly reduced implementation effort.

Currently Committed

A common problem in high-volume transaction environments involves read-only processes waiting until locks held by updating processes are released. DB2 has introduced many forms of lock avoidance over the years, and a further feature in DB2 10 provides additional flexibility.

The diagram in Figure 18 provides a typical example, with the **SELECT** process on the right waiting for the **DELETE** and **INSERT** processes on the left to complete and release their locks.

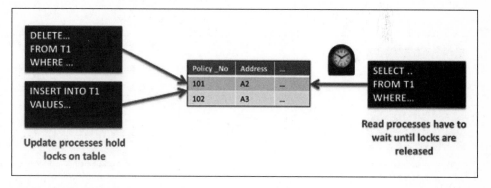

Figure 18: Typical lock wait scenario

Several releases ago, DB2 introduced the possibility of using "uncommitted read" semantics for read processes, to effectively ignore any locks held by other processes, as shown in Figure 19. However, by definition, such read processes could return inconsistent results: in the example, if the **DELETE** and **INSERT** were moving a sum of money between two bank accounts, it would be possible for the money to be counted twice, or not at all, by the **SELECT** process. Uncommitted read is therefore useful only in situations where the absolute consistency of the selected data is not important.

DB2 10 introduces a new way of specifying concurrency options for read processes that lets them access consistent data by ignoring an uncommitted **DELETE** or **INSERT** activity and reading the last committed version of rows in the table (Figure 20). Note that in its current implementation, currently committed applies to delete and insert activity only; read processes will still have to go through normal locking mechanisms for pending updates.

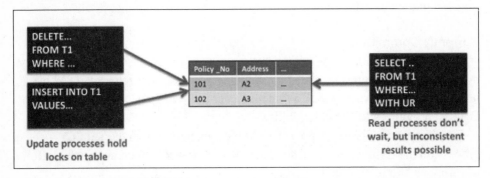

Figure 19: Use of uncommitted read

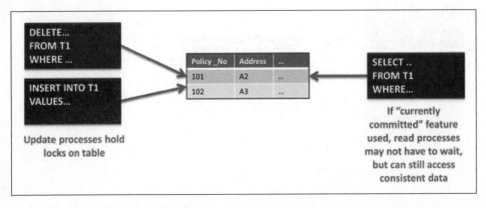

Figure 20: Use of currently committed

The currently committed behavior can be enabled on an application-by-application basis via a simple **BIND** parameter. As scalability limits are removed and DB2 supports ever-higher transaction volumes, improving application concurrency will become increasingly important. This feature is a significant step forward and brings DB2 in line with similar capabilities offered by several other relational databases.

Backup and Recovery Improvements

The combination of DB2 for z/OS and the underlying System z platform are undisputed in terms of resilience and security. However, situations do occur when database recovery is necessary, either as a result of human error or hardware or software failure. In such circumstances, it is of paramount business importance to reliably recover the affected data in the shortest possible time.

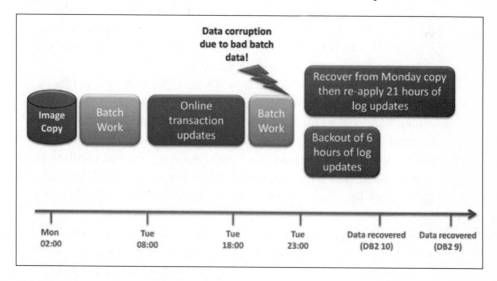

Figure 21: Backout vs. log apply recovery

As shown in Figure 21, for the first time DB2 gives DBAs the option of backing out changes in the event of a database recovery,[14] in addition to the more traditional recover/roll forward approach. In this example, incorrect input data to a batch process has corrupted the DB2 database.

In prior releases, the DBA would be forced to run a full recover to the point in time prior to the batch process, requiring all affected tables to be restored from the previous image copy and 21 hours of batch/online updates to be replayed from the DB2 log. With DB2 10's backout capability, the DBA could instead choose to undo the committed changes made by the offending batch process, resulting in a quicker overall recovery and less disruption/cost to the business.

Other related enhancements in DB2 10 remove some of the restrictions on use of FlashCopy[15] technology and provide more options for the production of "consistent" backups without impacting application availability.

Other Efficiency Enhancements

A number of other performance and productivity enhancements are delivered in DB2 10, including:

- *Distributed access optimizations.* DB2 is increasingly being called upon to act as a data server for distributed applications such as SAP. DB2 10 delivers a useful enhancement for incoming distributed requests involving a single-row **SELECT** using the **FETCH FIRST ROW ONLY** clause. By combining the open, fetch, and close sub-tasks into a single request, DB2 10 is able to more efficiently execute the instruction and reduce the amount of CPU and elapsed time consumed.

  Another enhancement in this area lets the DBA specify when the DB2 resources held by incoming distributed requests are released, via the **RELEASE** parameter of the package bind. For short OLTP-type distributed requests, this ability is expected to save significant CPU and elapsed time by preventing repeated de-allocation and re-allocation of DB2 packages each time a distributed request is received. Internal IBM testing has demonstrated CPU savings of 10 percent for this type of workload.

- *Native SQL procedure enhancements.* Stored procedures can be written in most of the programming languages commonly in use on the mainframe, but developers and DBAs also have the option to write stored procedures in native SQL (also known as Native SQL Procedures). Writing procedures in this language provides some significant benefits in application portability and maintenance as well as some cost/performance benefits. DB2 10 extends SQL procedure support to include some valuable new capabilities, such as the ability to accept XML objects as parameters and to use SQL scalar and table functions. These extensions improve DB2 10's consistency with DB2 for Linux®, UNIX®, and Windows® and other midrange databases, making it easier to port existing applications to DB2 for z/OS.

- *Improved zIIP exploitation.* DB2 10 lets some portions of the **RUNSTATS** utility, buffer pool prefetch, and deferred write processing to be offloaded to a zIIP specialty engine.[16] The amount of work from incoming distributed connections that can be offloaded to zIIP processors has also been increased so that up to 60 percent is now eligible. These changes can directly reduce the operational costs of eligible DB2 workloads.

- *Solid state disk (SSD) support.* DB2 10 supports the use of solid state disk drives. Although currently much more expensive per MB than traditional magnetic disk, SSDs are usually less expensive per I/O and provide some significant performance benefits. Placing certain DB2 objects on SSD (e.g., sort work files, high-performance tables that cannot be fully cached in memory) can dramatically reduce I/O times and improve performance.

- *Parallel index update at insert.* Applications generating a high volume of **INSERT** activity against a given DB2 table may encounter significant I/O delays due to the need to maintain multiple indexes in addition to the base table data. DB2 previously updated indexes sequentially, but in DB2 10 it is able to overlap the I/O operations for index updates, reducing the elapsed time for these processes. In common with other parallel activities, reduced elapsed time is usually achieved at the cost of an increase in overall CPU time, but in this case the overhead is very small and is eligible for offload to a zIIP engine if one is available.

- *Work file enhancements.* Work files are used to support joins and large sorts and are employed by a large proportion of most typical DB2 workloads. DB2 10 provides a number of enhancements in this area, including the ability to handle larger records (up to 64KB), optimizations for small sorts, and the ability to do more work in memory rather than externally on disk. Collectively, these improvements are expected to reduce CPU time and improve scalability.

- *Inline large objects.* Previously, DB2 large objects had to be stored in a separate table space from the conventional table data, requiring both locations to be accessed when LOB information was retrieved. DB2 10 allows part of the LOB to be stored "inline" within the base table, so that smaller LOBs (up to a few KB in size) can be retrieved without accessing the auxiliary table space, thereby improving performance and reducing CPU. One beta customer measured up to 80 percent CPU savings for **SELECT**s and 30 percent improvement for **INSERT** where the LOB can fit in the base table.

Resilience

The System z platform is rightly famed as one of the most robust and secure computing platforms on the planet. However, business and regulatory requirements in this area continue to get more demanding, so this is an important and ongoing focus area for the DB2 development team.

This section groups together some key new features that make DB2 more resilient to possible negative impacts of planned change, as well as increasing the flexibility and scope of the critical access control mechanisms that protect sensitive data from unauthorized access.

Plan Stability

One of the major headaches all DB2 users face when upgrading to a new release is the possibility of access path regression. In order to benefit from any enhancements to the optimizer (such as those covered in the discussions of CPU reductions and optimizer enhancements elsewhere in this paper), DB2 plans and packages typically need to be rebound under the new release.

The vast majority of the time, this will result in the same or better access path being selected (with a corresponding drop in CPU cost and elapsed time), but occasionally DB2 may select a worse one and performance suffers. Even though the risk of performance regression is usually small, it is enough to act as a serious disincentive, and many DB2 customers fail to exploit potential CPU reductions to avoid this risk. It is not unusual to see plans and packages that have not been rebound in the last 10 to 15 years at some sites.

Figure 22 illustrates this basic approach to access path management.

In an attempt to rectify this situation, DB2 9 introduced some new functionality in the maintenance stream[17] called Plan Stability. This enhancement provided some welcome new options for **REBIND** that allowed up to two old versions of a static SQL access path to be stored. If performance regression occurred following a **REBIND**, the previous access path could quickly and easily be re-established by running another **REBIND** using the **SWITCH** parameter. The diagram in Figure 23 illustrates this capability.

DB2 10 incorporates this enhancement into the base DB2 product code and enhances it to allow any number of previous access paths to be stored.

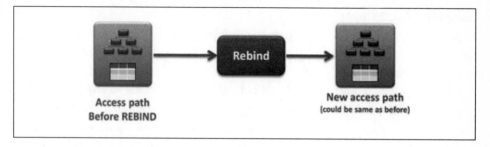

Figure 22: DB2 with no plan stability

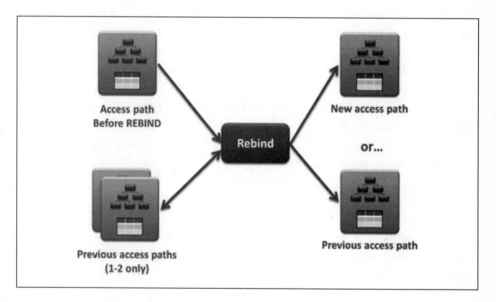

Figure 23: DB2 9 plan stability

Plan stability removes the majority of the risk associated with rebinding static packages following any DB2 upgrade, allowing more customers to exploit more of the performance enhancements delivered in each release. Those customers that have not rebound their plans/packages for a considerable time may see very significant benefits, as they are able to exploit several releases worth of optimizer enhancements at once.

Enhanced Audit Capabilities

Many legal compliance and business requirements involve the creation of a detailed audit log for sensitive data held within DB2. Although previous versions of DB2 did have an audit capability, it had a number of serious flaws—the most significant of which allowed DB2 to audit only the first access to any given table within a single transaction, with all subsequent accesses not being recorded on the audit log.

DB2 10 provides a long-awaited solution in the shape of a formal audit policy. This new feature is flexible enough to allow specific tables to be monitored for specific periods and includes a record of *all* relevant SQL activity within a given transaction, including read and update activity. Wildcarding is supported to allow a single audit rule to cover multiple tables, and distributed identity support allows the "real" user ID passed by distributed applications such as SAP to be recorded in the audit record.

The new audit capabilities in DB2 10 address some long-overdue short-comings in the functionality provided by previous DB2 releases and will give auditors the means to track and report on all significant access to sensitive DB2 data without having to resort to external packages or expensive application coding.

More Flexible Administrative Authorities

Many DB2 customers go to great lengths to ensure that access to sensitive DB2 data is limited to users who have a business requirement to be able to read and update it. However, many of the DB2 system authorities[18] necessary for DB2 systems programmers and DBAs to do their jobs also implicitly have given them read and write access to all the data in the system. Additional processes have therefore been required to audit the activities conducted under these authorities.

DB2 10 introduces a number of new system authorities designed to allow proper separation of administration and data access. These authorities are built around specific roles in a typical DB2 environment, as follows:

- *Security Administrator.* The new **SECADM** authority allows all security-related administration tasks (granting and revoking data access, setting up roles, and so on) to be conducted by a security administrator without having to provide **SYSADM** super-user privileges. The traditional security privileges held by **SYSADM** can be removed when this option is enabled.

- *System Database Administrator.* DBAs can now be given a new **SYSTEM DBADM** authority (allowing them to make schema and structure changes to all databases) with or without implicitly being given the ability to access the underlying data (or give others access). Previously, **DBADM** had to be provided individually for each database and implicitly allowed data access.
- *Data Administrator.* The new **DATAACCESS** authority provides access to all data within a subsystem without the ability to structurally change any of the DB2 objects.
- *Performance Specialist.* Staff responsible for monitoring and tuning SQL need to be able to investigate access paths via the **EXPLAIN** facility, manage performance traces, and update DB2 statistics. The new **SQLADM** authority provides this set of abilities, without being able to access any underlying user data access or change any DB2 database structures.
- *Developer.* The new **EXPLAIN** privilege lets developers check the access path DB2 will use for critical SQL statements without needing to have access to the underlying data being accessed within the SQL.

Established DB2 sites will have to carefully evaluate their use of existing DB2 system authorities before being able to exploit these new capabilities. However, this increased flexibility will allow many sites to reduce their use of the all-powerful **SYSADM** authority and make it considerably easier to address many of the concerns commonly raised when auditing access to sensitive DB2 data.

Improved Data Access Control

DB2 access has traditionally been granted at the table level. Where more granular access was required (allowing access to only a subset of the columns or rows in a table), this had to be implemented within each application, or an awkward view mechanism had to be used. Figure 24 illustrates such a situation, where the manager has full read/write access to a table containing sensitive data, but a view has had to be defined on the table to limit access for normal users to the non-sensitive columns.

Recent versions of DB2 have expanded these choices by providing sophisticated multi-level security mechanisms to meet exacting military standards. However, this approach can be complex to understand and implement, and it lacks flexibility.

DB2 10 introduces new capabilities for row- and column-level access control, which are fully integrated into the database engine and defined using standard SQL constructs.

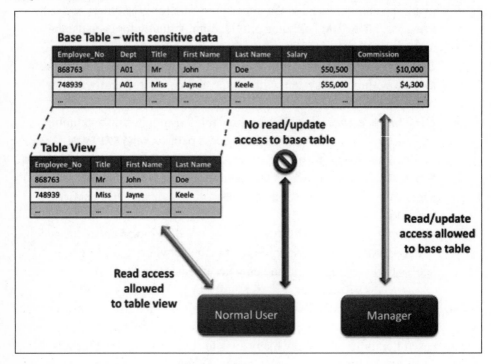

Figure 24: Traditional row/column control via views

At the row level, a policy can be created to filter rows from the table based on the role/authorities of the requesting user. The row policy applies to **INSERT**, **UPDATE**, and **DELETE** statements in addition to **SELECT**. Similarly, a column policy can be created to mask certain sensitive column values, including subsets of the column. As these policies are integrated at the table level, they are transparent to all the applications accessing the data and are universally and consistently enforced.

Figure 25 shows an example of these new capabilities within a DB2 10 environment. The same table is now protected by a column access policy that allows only managers to see the **SALARY** and **COMMISSION** columns in the table.

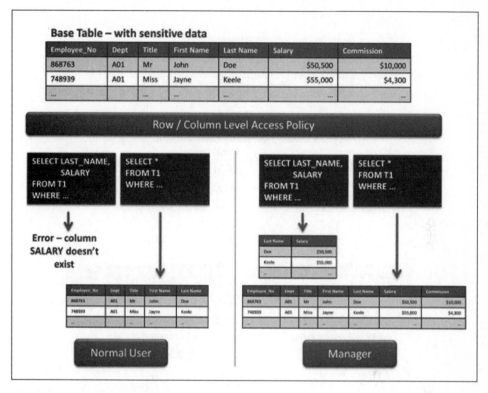

Figure 25: DB2 10 column policy

Based on the restrictions defined in the policy, normal users will not be able to see the sensitive columns (and will in fact receive an error saying that the column doesn't exist if they try to select it explicitly). In comparison, a manager will have full access to all columns.

Extensions to this same approach provide data-masking capabilities using the same policies. In the example shown in Figure 26, all digits of a credit card number except the last four are masked with an "X" character for normal users, but authorized users are automatically allowed to see the full number.

These enhancements finally allow security logic to be fully separated from application logic, providing significant additional flexibility and ensuring consistent security behavior regardless of the mechanism used to access the data. Subsequent changes to security can then be implemented independently without having to change any application logic, reducing implementation cost and improving developer productivity.

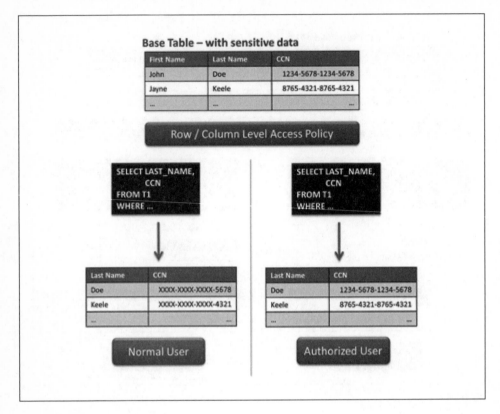

Figure 26: DB2 10 column masking

Improved Dynamic Schema Change

The enhancements to DB2's dynamic schema change capabilities (as described elsewhere in this document) are also relevant in terms of resilience. Each of the new capabilities eliminates a requirement to unload, drop, re-create, and reload data that would otherwise be required in order to implement the schema change. This, in turn, increases data availability while also increasing resilience due to the lower likelihood of human error leading to temporary or permanent loss of data.

Temporal Data

As described in the discussion of temporal tables, this important new facility allows DB2 to maintain a full transaction history for specified tables and enables developers to code elegant SQL queries to determine the state of a given row at any point in the past.

In addition to addressing fundamental line-of-business requirements for maintaining a history of a given business object, temporal tables can help to address regulatory requirements. The ability to more rapidly respond to such requirements and deliver the necessary audit/history trail, while expending fewer person-hours in coding and testing applications, will be a valuable business benefit for many large enterprises.

Growth

Supporting workload growth, both in terms of increased scalability/throughput and catering to new types of workload, remains a key focus area for the DB2 for z/OS development team.

Despite the recent global economic slowdown, large DB2 customers around the world continue to experience ever-increasing transaction and data volumes, with DB2 for z/OS being asked to shoulder much of the load. Each release of DB2 must continue to significantly expand DB2's limits in order to cope with this demand.

At the same time, DB2's role as an enterprise data server means that it is called upon to support an ever more diverse set of workloads. New classes of data, such as XML, place unique demands on the database engine, while an increasing focus on hosting business intelligence and advanced analytics applications on the System z platform is driving a new generation of hardware and software solutions.

This section addresses the new DB2 10 features aimed at supporting these demands.

Increased Scalability Through Full 64-bit Exploitation

In an effort to drive down IT costs and deliver better value, customers everywhere are constantly trying to do more with less. They want fewer machines to manage and fewer databases to care for, and they want to support larger and more complex workloads without an associated increase in IT staff. These drivers mean that there is constant pressure to increase the amount of work a DB2 system can handle.

Storage constraints remain the single biggest factor in limiting the scalability of a single DB2 system today. Each process that runs concurrently within that system requires some storage, so the more workload a given system is asked to handle, the higher the storage requirements.

In DB2 V8, IBM embarked upon a major project to transform DB2 into a 64-bit RDBMS, removing many of the addressability issues inherent in the previous 31-bit memory model (Figure 27).

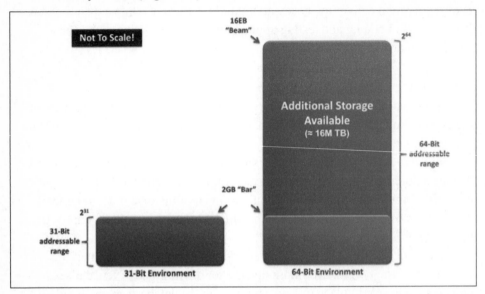

Figure 27: 64-bit memory model

DB2 V8 also moved several key storage areas above the 2GB "bar" into the newly addressable memory space, relieving some of the storage constraints and allowing more workload per DB2 subsystem. DB2 9 increased scalability by a further 10 to 15 percent by moving another set of storage areas above the bar. But even with those enhancements, most customers have been limited to running a maximum of 300 to 500 concurrent active connections within each DB2 system. As we saw in Figure 4, this often meant paying a performance and productivity penalty by increasing the number of DB2 systems needed to run a given workload.

In DB2 10, IBM has completed the bulk of the remaining work in the 64-bit migration effort, with 80 to 90 percent of the remaining DB2 storage structures moving above the bar. This has enabled a spectacular increase in the number of threads that can be supported by a single subsystem—most customers will be able to achieve 5 to 10 times the number of concurrent connections compared with DB2 9. In addition to the cost and performance benefits described earlier, this vastly improves DB2's ability to support very high-volume workloads. However, the ability to run such a large number of threads within a single DB2 system is bound to expose new bottlenecks, and IBM has already begun to address these (see the discussions on DB2 catalog enhancements and other growth enhancements elsewhere in this document for examples).

pureXML Enhancements

DB2 9 introduced pureXML to DB2 for z/OS: a major new feature that allowed XML documents to be stored natively within DB2 and easily retrieved using the power of SQL and XPath. Some significant performance improvements have since been delivered via the DB2 9 service stream, but DB2 10 introduces several additional enhancements to pureXML functionality, including:

XML schema validation. Although XML is a universal interchange format capable of representing almost any form of data, it is possible to define a schema that limits the structure and content of specific XML documents. The process of ensuring that a given XML document adheres to a given schema is known as schema validation, and DB2 10 includes a new built-in function to support this important task. The function is capable of automatically determining the relevant XML schema for validation, and it makes schema validation 100 percent eligible for offload to a zIIP processor if available. This feature promises to improve developer productivity and reduce CPU costs for this important XML process.

Partial update. The initial implementation of pureXML required that a complete XML document be replaced if it needed to be updated. No support was provided for updating just a part of the XML document, known as a "node" (Figure 28).

DB2 10 addresses this issue by providing support for partial document update, allowing individual nodes within a document to be added, changed, or removed. Figure 29 illustrates this capability.

This enhancement will significantly reduce the amount of log data written for updates to large XML documents, improving performance and reducing CPU and elapsed times.

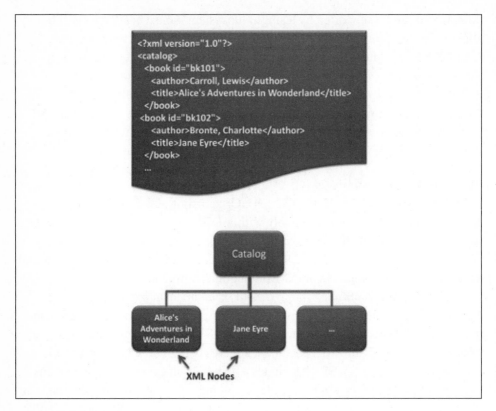

Figure 28: Sample XML document

Binary XML format. DB2 10 introduces a new binary XML format that can be used for more efficiently passing XML documents between a client application and DB2. This can dramatically reduce the size of XML documents and has resulted in CPU and elapsed time reductions ranging from 10 to 30 percent in internal IBM tests.

CHECK DATA *support.* The **CHECK DATA** utility can be used against conventional DB2 data to ensure that the table data is consistent with any associated indexes and related tables. DB2 10 extends support to include XML documents, so that users can ensure that all nodes in an XML document are well-formed, internally consistent, and valid.

Other pureXML enhancements. Additional pureXML features delivered in DB2 10 include improved indexing support for XML columns and enhanced support for user-defined functions (UDFs) and for triggers and stored procedures.

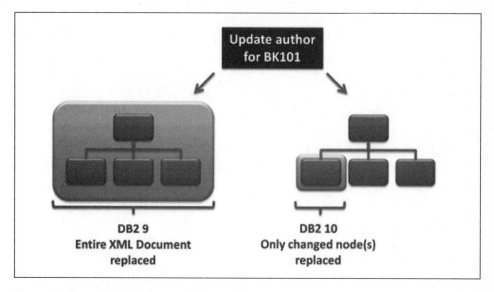

Figure 29: Sample XML document with partial update

Collectively, these enhancements address the major functional and operational issues encountered by users of the initial pureXML support delivered in DB2 9, while improving consistency with other members of the DB2 family and improving both developer and DBA productivity.

DB2 Catalog Enhancements

The Catalog[19] is one of the most vital components in any DB2 system. It contains a set of tables and internal structures that represent all the metadata necessary for the subsystem to operate, and it is used extensively by nearly every DB2 process from application programs to DBAs creating a new database. DB2 10 includes some important enhancements to the Catalog, including:

Standard UTS format. In previous releases, the catalog used a non-standard internal storage format and maintained links between the various tables using special internal pointers. DB2 10 converts some key Catalog structures to use the standard Universal Table Space partition-by growth (UTS PBG) format introduced in DB2 9 (see the Appendix). This change allows standard online **REORG** processes to be used against the catalog, improving performance and availability compared with previous releases.

Contention between various processes needing to read/update the Catalog can cause significant operational disruption. As part of the same change, the converted Catalog tables have been spread across many more table spaces than before, and row-level locking has been implemented to allow DB2 10 to support much higher levels of current access than were previously possible.

Maximum Catalog size. Many DB2 subsystems have to support hundreds of thousands of database objects. Each of these objects must be recorded in the DB2 Catalog, and in some cases the 64GB limit for certain components, such as the **SPT01** table space, can be a scalability limitation.

DB2 10 addresses the 64GB limitation on **SPT01** by moving some large columns into large object (LOB) columns. This makes use of the inline LOB support added in DB2 10 (discussed elsewhere in this document), making the Catalog tables more readable and allowing more packages to be supported within a single DB2 system.

Other Growth Enhancements

DB2 10 includes a number of other enhancements designed to improve scalability and support future workload growth, including:

Latch and **UTSERIAL** *contention relief.* A latch is an internal DB2 lock on an object, taken to ensure only one process updates a given resource at any one time. As overall workload increases, latches can become an increasingly important factor in limiting DB2 throughput. DB2 10 includes some optimizations to reduce latching delays for many routine DB2 processes, such as logging and accessing buffer pool pages. The **UTSERIAL** lock taken by DB2 utilities has also been removed, permitting greater concurrency for compatible utilities.

Currently committed. This new locking mechanism should significantly increase the concurrency of some read-only workloads that are currently unable to make use of the older uncommitted read protocol.

Extended Address Volumes (EAV) support. With today's advanced storage management subsystems, traditional concepts such as physical DASD "volumes" are being transformed into purely logical constructs capable of supporting much higher capacities. z/OS 1.10, 1.11, and 1.12 introduced and subsequently enhanced support for EAVs, allowing up to 262,668 cylinders per logical volume (approximately 180GB). DB2 10 includes changes for EAV support,[20] allowing fewer volumes to be defined and reducing administrative overheads.

TIMESTAMP *enhancements.* DB2 10 extends the precision of the **TIMESTAMP** data type to support fractions of a second from zero up to 12 digits of precision (the previous precision was fixed at six digits). This enhancement provides greater flexibility, and the increased precision enables timestamps to be used as unique identifiers for certain tables with a much lower risk of duplicates being generated.

Timestamp with time zone. DB2 10 also introduces a new SQL data type called **TIMESTAMP WITH TIMEZONE**. This data type is able to store time zone information in addition to the standard timestamp data, with DB2 handling the necessary conversion to UTC[21] for timestamp comparisons and arithmetic. This feature enhances DB2's ability to support applications used in multiple time zones.

Business Analytics

Traditionally, DB2 for z/OS was considered to be primarily an OLTP data server, with the DB2 for Linux, UNIX, and Windows variant (or other vendor databases) being a more common choice for analytics and data warehousing duties. Cost concerns or historical inertia has often dictated this approach, but the superior resilience and scalability of the System z platform, combined with the increasing popularity of real-time warehousing, is leading many customers to re-examine this decision.

DB2 9 delivered some significant new functionality to support business analytics workloads, including improvements to indexing, query optimization, and SQL extensions. This emphasis continues within DB2 10, with a large number of new and enhanced features, both within the DB2 product itself and within the supporting tools and infrastructure.

Enhanced OLAP SQL Functionality

Online Analytical Processing (OLAP) is used to allow analysis of multi-dimensional sets of data to provide new business insights. For example, sales data (typically represented by a cube) might be analyzed to determine whether a particular branch, product, or brand is performing well.

DB2 10 introduces support for moving sums, averages, and aggregates, extending the OLAP SQL functionality previously delivered in DB2 9. Figure 30 shows an example of some SQL using the new moving average functionality to display sales figures for each region in a sales history table.

These new SQL constructs allow DB2 to more efficiently process common OLAP queries within the database engine, reducing the cost and elapsed time associated with extracting large volumes of data for analysis within the OLAP tool itself.

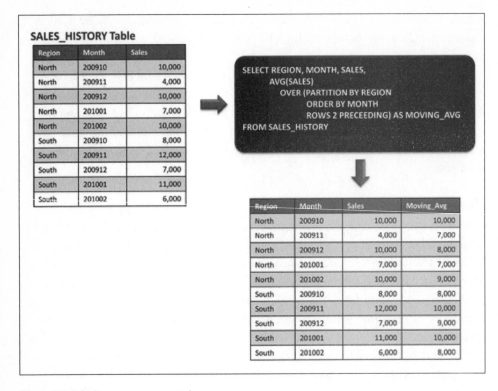

SALES_HISTORY Table

Region	Month	Sales
North	200910	10,000
North	200911	4,000
North	200912	10,000
North	201001	7,000
North	201002	10,000
South	200910	8,000
South	200911	12,000
South	200912	7,000
South	201001	11,000
South	201002	6,000

```
SELECT REGION, MONTH, SALES,
    AVG(SALES)
        OVER (PARTITION BY REGION
            ORDER BY MONTH
            ROWS 2 PRECEEDING) AS MOVING_AVG
FROM SALES_HISTORY
```

Region	Month	Sales	Moving_Avg
North	200910	10,000	10,000
North	200911	4,000	7,000
North	200912	10,000	8,000
North	201001	7,000	7,000
North	201002	10,000	9,000
South	200910	8,000	8,000
South	200911	12,000	10,000
South	200912	7,000	9,000
South	201001	11,000	10,000
South	201002	6,000	8,000

Figure 30: Moving average example

IBM Smart Analytics Optimizer

As DB2 for z/OS becomes more attractive as a host for large-scale analytics and analytics workloads, the requirement to deliver high performance with minimal administration and tuning overheads increases accordingly. In recognition of this trend, IBM has developed an innovative solution that combines DB2 for z/OS and a dedicated blade server capable of executing the complex queries typically found in analytics/analytics applications with fast and predictable response times. Known as the IBM Smart Analytics Optimizer,[22] this solution is deeply integrated with DB2 10[23] and allows DB2 to offload eligible query components to the locally attached blade as shown in Figure 31.

This architecture is able to deliver up to 10X performance gains for qualifying queries[24] when compared with traditional DB2 processing. As the DB2 optimizer decides what work to offload to the appliance, no application changes are required in order to take advantage of the Smart Analytics Optimizer once it is made available.

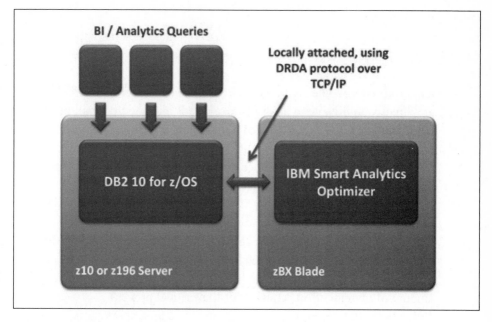

Figure 31: Smart Analytics Optimizer architecture

Query Management Facility

IBM's Query Management Facility (QMF) tool is as old as DB2 itself and provides a solid platform for executing many customer's analytics and analytics queries. QMF 10, which will be released at the same time as DB2 10 for z/OS, provides many new or enhanced facilities, including:

- Integrated infrastructure, supporting the full spectrum of analytics capabilities, from table data editing and ad hoc querying to graphical reporting and interactive visual dashboards
- BI content that can be deployed to both workstation- and browser-based users
- Programming-free, drag-and-drop authoring model
- Rich, graphical reports with a wide variety of output choices, including Microsoft® Excel®, HTML, PDF, and others
- Interactive dashboards with the ability to present data drawn concurrently from multiple heterogeneous data sources
- Business Intelligence and Reporting Tools (BIRT) report-format support

Other Enhancements

A large number of the previously described DB2 10 enhancements will also directly benefit typical analytics/warehousing workloads. These include:

- *CPU reductions.* The significant CPU reductions described earlier are directly applicable to analytics workloads and should result in an immediate CPU/cost reduction of 5 to 10 percent for most environments.
- *Temporal tables.* This functionality should prove very valuable in warehousing/analysis environments, which commonly have to support a historical perspective.
- *Automatic statistics collection.* Most analytics environments consist of many hundreds or thousands of tables, many of which are growing rapidly over time. In this kind of environment, maintaining up-to-date database statistics is essential to allow DB2 to continue to use the correct access path. DB2 10's new automatic statistics facilities will reduce the amount of manual effort required for this critical process.
- *Index **INCLUDE**.* Analytics environments have to support complex query workloads against large data volumes, which makes it necessary to have good indexing in place on key tables. The index **INCLUDE** enhancement described previously could help to reduce the number of indexes needed in environments, with an associated reduction in the cost of regularly loading data into the warehouse.
- *Buffer pool enhancements.* Many analytics environments require large buffer pools to support efficient access to large data volumes. The buffer pool enhancements in DB2 10 will reduce the costs associated with buffer pool access for analytics applications.
- *Optimizer enhancements.* Analytics queries are frequently complex and access large amounts of data. The DB2 optimizer enhancements outlined previously will help many such queries to complete more quickly, and with less CPU.

Overall, these enhancements further enhance DB2's analytics credentials on the System z platform and make it significantly more attractive from a cost and functionality perspective. Preliminary IBM measurements show an average 20 percent CPU reduction from a TPC-H–like[25] workload using 150 queries.

Section III

Upgrading to DB2 10

This section outlines some of the considerations around the timing and structure of the DB2 10 upgrade process.

Skip Migration

Traditionally, IBM has supported migration to a new release of DB2 only from the release immediately preceding it (you could migrate to DB2 9 only from a Version 8 subsystem, for example). Up until now, the only recent exception to this rule was DB2 for z/OS V7, which supported direct migration from both Version 5 and Version 6. There were good reasons for IBM to offer this facility in 2001 when Version 7 became Generally Available, as "Y2K fever" had prevented many Version 5 customers from being able to migrate to Version 6 according to their usual timescales. Skip migration was a good way to help those customers catch up and reposition themselves to stay current as subsequent releases became available, but it wasn't without its downsides: it required IBM to expend significant additional effort to develop and support, and it left customers with twice the number of prerequisites to manage and new function to absorb.

With DB2 10, IBM will once again support skip migration, allowing Version 8 as well as DB2 9 systems to be migrated to DB2 10, and for very similar reasons to those that convinced IBM to support the jump from Version 5 to Version 7 way back in 2001. Despite DB2 9 containing some very attractive new function and being Generally Available since 2007, the recent global economic downturn has seriously impacted IT budgets, and many customers still find themselves running DB2 V8 (or even earlier releases).

However, the availability of the skip migration feature does not mean that all DB2 customers currently on Version 8 should wait and go directly to DB2 10. As mentioned above, skip migrations do have some downsides in terms of increased complexity and risk, and the amount of planning and implementation effort required for a Version 8 to Version 10 upgrade is greater than that needed for a single-release upgrade (although still less than that needed for two separate upgrades).

If you're on Version 8 today, chances are you're missing out on some significant business benefits that DB2 9 for z/OS could provide, including some modest

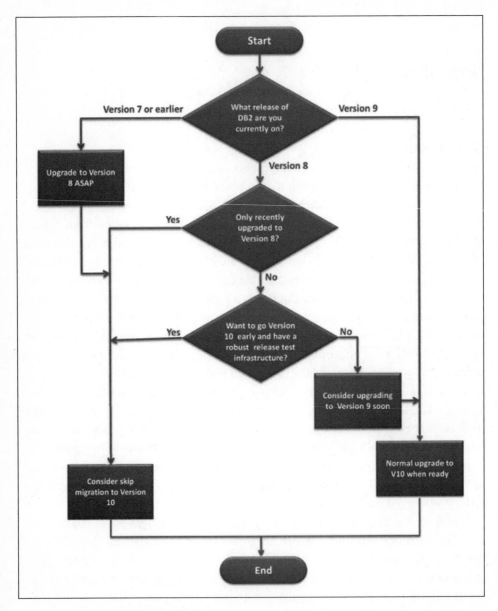

Figure 32: DB2 10 upgrade decision process

CPU savings for most workloads. If you need to move from Version 8 before you are ready for DB2 10, then moving to DB2 9 provides solid value now.

Skip migration is primarily intended to support three scenarios:

- Customers who are still running DB2 V7 and have yet to complete their upgrade to DB2 V8. Most of those will be planning an upgrade to Version 8 very soon, but Version 8 upgrade projects typically take at least 6 to 12 months to fully roll out. Once the Version 8 upgrade process is complete, those customers will be well placed to take advantage of the skip migration feature and go directly to DB2 10.
- Customers that have only just completed their Version 7 to Version 8 upgrade project and are unlikely to get business approval for another migration to DB2 9 so soon after the last one. These customers may want to consider staying with Version 8 for now and migrating directly to DB2 10 during the next 18 to 24 months.
- Customers who have usually migrated quickly to new versions but did not move to DB2 9. If customers usually start working with new versions in the first year, they have tests and processes for dealing with the normal maturity pattern. These customers may be able to skip DB2 9 and deliver more value in a shorter timescale.

Figure 32 summarizes this decision-making process.

To reduce the financial impact of running two versions of DB2 concurrently, IBM may offer eligible customers a Single Version Charging[26] option for a period of up to 18 months when migrating directly from Version 8 to DB2 10.

Whichever path is taken, it is important for DB2 customers to ensure that they get good advice about the advantages and disadvantages of each option. In particular, the effort involved in a skip migration should not be underestimated, and the "culture shock" for developers and support staff asked to take on two releases worth of new function in a single bound can be considerable.

DB2 V8 Support

IBM recently announced that support for DB2 for z/OS V8 will formally end on April 30, 2012. For many DB2 customers that have strict policies prohibiting the use of out-of-support software for mission-critical systems, this will clarify the timescales for their DB2 10 upgrade process.

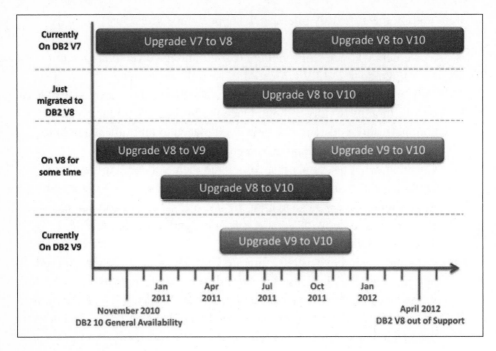

Figure 33: Possible DB2 upgrade timescales

Using the decision process outlined in the preceding figure, organizations just about to migrate to DB2 V8 have around 18 months from the date this paper was written to complete the Version 8 upgrade and then to plan and implement their skip migration to DB2 10. Given the typical timescales involved with upgrade projects, these organizations need to begin planning the Version 8 upgrade immediately if they are going to complete the DB2 10 upgrade before Version 8 support is withdrawn in April 2012. Extended service for six months is being offered to customers who are skipping from Version 8 to DB2 10.

Figure 33 shows some possible upgrade timescales for DB2 customers based on their current position.

Section IV

DB2 10 Customer Case Studies

This section is based upon interviews with some of the organizations that participated in the DB2 10 beta program. Based on their early experiences with the product, they outline the business benefits they expect by exploiting the features in the new release.

Case Study #1: Banco do Brasil

The Banco do Brasil is the oldest and largest active bank in Brazil and one of the longest-established financial institutions in the world. However, its IT infrastructure is definitely of the modern variety, and DB2 for z/OS sits right at the heart of its critical banking systems. With over 40 million clients in 22 countries around the world, coping with ever-increasing transaction volumes and an absolute need for 24x7 availability is a constant technology challenge.

Despite the virtual storage savings provided by DB2 9 for z/OS, the bank currently has to employ a 20-way data sharing group to handle its main production workload, with the DB2 members being spread over six physical z10 servers. Even with 20 DB2 subsystems sharing the load, constant and careful virtual storage monitoring is required to maintain availability.

"With the scalability improvements in DB2 10, we expect to be able to quickly reduce our production data sharing group from 20 members to 15," says Paulo Sahadi, Senior Production Manager, Information Management Division at Banco do Brasil. With DB2 10 able to handle five to 10 times as many threads as the previous version, the upgrade will immediately give the bank some much-needed room for future workload growth while simultaneously reducing its data sharing overhead. "We will also save some CPU and storage from removing the five DB2 systems, and we will have to spend a lot less time monitoring our virtual storage," Paulo adds.

Banco do Brasil also expects to see some significant business benefits from DB2 10's parallel index update enhancement, as many of its most demanding workloads involve heavy concurrent insert activity against tables with several indexes. "This will reduce the elapsed time for some of our most critical processes," says Paulo, "delivering a more responsive application and allowing us to sustain greater throughput."

Today's banking customers expect to be able to access their accounts 24 hours a day, so maintaining data availability is a very important consideration when scheduling routine housekeeping activities. To avoid any potential impact on business transactions, Paulo's team is currently forced to defer the execution of many activities, such as schema changes and **REBIND**s, and run them in tightly defined windows on weekends. "The restructured catalog in DB2 10 will greatly reduce the impact of these routine processes and allow us to run them during the week so we can be more responsive to the requirements of the business," adds Paulo.

Banco do Brasil has an unwavering focus on maintaining the availability and stability of its critical IT systems. In a testament to the robustness of the beta code and the compelling business advantages offered by the new release, the bank is considering beginning the DB2 10 upgrade process as early as the second half of 2011, with the intention of moving all systems to DB2 10 new function mode within another 12 to 18 months.

Overall, Paulo is pleased with what he has seen so far in the bank's beta testing. "DB2 10 enhances our ability to support our rapidly growing workloads while delivering some very valuable new function with immediate business benefits."

Case Study #2: BMW Group

As one of the world's most successful car manufacturers, the BMW Group is at the forefront of both automotive and IT innovation. DB2 for z/OS is a critical component of many of the company's worldwide computer systems, from manufacturing to supplier management and customer ordering. In total, the car company has around 130 DB2 subsystems, belonging to over 40 data sharing groups.

BMW completed its migration to DB2 9 in June 2009, and although it saw some significant benefits from the upgrade, it also encountered some challenges with access path selection in that release. Philipp Nowak, BMW DB2 Product Manager involved in the upgrade, takes up the story: "With our DB2 10 testing so far, we have had quite a few surprises, but all of them have been good. Every single SQL statement we have tested has been better or the same as our current optimal paths—we have yet to see any significant access path regression. We had to spend a lot of time tuning SQL with DB2 9, but we expect that to disappear when we upgrade to DB2 10."

BMW has also been evaluating the concurrent **INSERT** enhancements in DB2 10, as this is an important part of many of its critical production workloads. "We have measured a 38 percent reduction in CPU and a 7 percent reduction in suspend time for some heavy insert workloads in a data sharing environment," says Philipp. "That's a significant saving which provides immediate business benefit."

Philipp also expects to see significant benefits from the z/OS large page support in DB2 10. "We use very large buffer pools—some of them up to 3.2GB in size," he says. "Our systems have to support lots of different workloads at the same time, including users connecting directly, for example, via Excel ODBC, so buffer pool performance is very important for us. We rely on efficient access to buffered data, and any saving in the cost of accessing that data will be very beneficial."

In common with many other organizations, BMW is constantly striving to minimize the costs of its IT operations. "We expect the virtual storage enhancements in DB2 10 to allow us to reduce in the production environment the number of DB2 group members we run," says Peter Paetsch, an external DB2 Consultant. "That will reduce the amount of time we spend in monitoring virtual storage usage and will decrease our data sharing overheads, too."

What other DB2 10 features will BMW find particularly valuable? "The new catalog structure will help to reduce the operational pain of normal activities during the daily business, such as package rebinds," says Philipp. "Although we're only in the early stages of investigating the technology, the pureXML enhancements in DB2 10 for special applications also look very useful," adds Peter.

So, how would the BMW DB2 team sum up its experiences with DB2 10 during the beta program? "Overall, we are very pleased with the added functionality and architectural enhancements and are looking forward to this exciting release," reports Philipp.

Section V

Summary

Even in the most favorable economic climate, businesses need to control costs and increase efficiency to improve their bottom line. In today's more challenging business environment, this has become a key factor for the survival and success of enterprises of all sizes.

DB2 10 delivers significant "out of the box" benefits that many customers will be able to exploit with little or no additional effort. These include the most aggressive performance and CPU improvements of any DB2 release in the past 20 years, scalability enhancements to support ever-increasing workloads, and productivity improvements to allow DB2 developers and support staff to respond more rapidly to the demands of the business.

Collectively, these features deliver real and quantifiable business benefit, and many customers will be considering upgrading to DB2 10 much more quickly than they may have done for previous releases.

DB2 10 delivers significant "out of the box" benefits that many customers will be able to exploit with little or no additional effort. These include the most aggressive performance and CPU improvements of any DB2 release in the past 20 years, scalability enhancements to support ever-increasing workloads, and productivity improvements to allow DB2 developers and support staff to respond more rapidly to the demands of the business.

Appendix

DB2 9 Review

Today, DB2 is universally accepted as the premier database system for IBM's System z mainframe architecture. Although other products do exist for this platform, DB2 sits at the heart of most of the business-critical mainframe IT applications that have been written during the past 20 years.

DB2 9 has been Generally Available since March 2007, and a significant amount of the DB2 worldwide workload is now running on that release. The scalability and reliability of IBM's zSeries platform make it a very attractive choice for customers' high-volume, mission-critical applications.

This appendix briefly reviews DB2 9 and looks at some of the ways in which it helps to deliver competitive edge. For a more detailed review of DB2 9, see the 2007 Triton white paper *DB2 9 for z/OS – Data on Demand.*[27]

Support for New Workloads

The demands being placed upon enterprise data stores are continually expanding. Many modern business applications have moved beyond the processing of traditional "structured" data and now have to deal with new types such as XML and binary data (including images, audio, and video). Databases have to handle these new data types while continuing to provide the same levels of performance, resilience, and security that customers have come to rely on.

At the same time, IBM continues to evolve the mainframe platform and extend the range of applications it is able to efficiently support. Running ERP and business analytics applications on the System z platform is becoming increasingly popular as specific new function is added to DB2 (and other system software) to support them. New features delivered in DB2 9 in support of these new workloads include:

Integrated XML. The pureXML feature provides a full-fledged XML storage engine within DB2, letting XML documents be easily stored in their native format while retaining DB2's traditional strengths for structured relational data. XPath and SQL can be used interchangeably (or in combination) to query XML and relational data. This provides immediate flexibility and productivity advantages, with traditional application developers able to query both relational and XML data with SQL, while XML specialists are able to use the power of XPath to access the same data.

Large object support. DB2 for z/OS has supported large objects (LOBs) for some time, but some significant restrictions made it difficult for many customers to make use of these features. Most of these restrictions are addressed in DB2 9, with enhanced utility support, more efficient LOB retrieval, and a revised locking model. These enhancements make DB2 9 a more attractive host for LOB data and will allow a greater range of applications to take advantage of the resilience and security offered by DB2.

Native SQL procedures. Stored procedures can provide a number of significant benefits, including lower maintenance costs, better performance, and enhanced security. DB2 9 lets SQL stored procedures be executed natively by DB2, removing the need for a z/OS C compiler and improving performance by up to 80 percent compared with Version 8. Additional enhancements to versioning and deployment facilities for SQL stored procedures significantly broaden both the scope and appeal of SQL procedures, letting them be deployed more efficiently and executed more quickly and at lower cost than before.

Enhanced ERP support. DB2 for z/OS is well established as the premier data server for high-end ERP systems such as SAP, and Version 9 delivers a large number of enhancements specifically designed to improve support for these workloads. These include new ways of partitioning tables, improvements to table row formats, and volume-based utilities. Together, these enhancements reduce DB2 CPU usage and improve DBA productivity and data availability. They further consolidate DB2's position as the preferred database for ERP applications such as SAP.

Business analytics. Many customers are considering the advantages of DB2 for z/OS as an analytics platform, and DB2 9 provides some welcome enhancements in this area. These include indexing improvements, extensions to SQL, and optimizer enhancements, all of which significantly enhance DB2's analytics credentials on the System z platform and underline IBM's renewed emphasis in this area.

Streamlined Security and Compliance

Compliance is one of the major business challenges facing today's enterprises, and nowhere is that challenge more keenly felt than within IT. Regulations such as the Sarbanes-Oxley Act, HIPAA, and Basel II place serious and demanding obligations on companies to protect and secure the sensitive information held within their IT systems, and to be able to prove that they have done so.

The System z platform has a long history of providing a safe and secure environment for data, but these new regulations have raised requirements for new features within the operating system and other system software. DB2 9 has responded to these requirements with the following enhancements:

Network trusted contexts and roles. DB2 9 introduces the concept of network trusted contexts: predefined incoming connections that originate from a trusted location and are therefore able to bypass normal authentication checks and reduce overhead. In the meantime, normal DB2 security rules will remain in place for non-trusted connections. This approach provides the best of both worlds, with robust security for non-trusted connections and good accountability with no performance compromises for trusted connections. Another new DB2 9 feature allows a set of DB2 privileges to be grouped into a construct known as a role. Together, these two new features provide significantly enhanced security, better auditability, and improved performance when compared with previous versions of DB2.

Enhanced auditing. The ability to audit changes made to data, and to the access given to that data, is a key aspect of many compliance regulations. DB2's audit capabilities have also been enhanced to encompass the role concept described above. DB2 9 also makes it possible to be much more selective when starting audit (and other) traces, letting you confine tracing to those areas where it is required and reducing the volume and overhead of trace data.

Instead-of triggers. A commonly used technique for limiting application access to sensitive tables in DB2 is to use a view on the table that excludes the sensitive information and give the application access only to the view. This approach works well for read access, but under some conditions it is not possible to perform inserts, updates, or deletes through a view. Instead-of triggers avoid this issue by allowing an alternative action to be specified when an update operation is attempted against a view. This in turn removes the requirement to allow any sort of direct access to the sensitive table, thereby improving security.

SSL support and encryption. One of the great strengths of DB2 for z/OS has always been its ability to rapidly exploit advances in the underlying hardware and operating system. DB2 9 continues this trend by supporting the use of System z disk and tape controllers to encrypt data. Many organizations are required to encrypt their DB2 data for compliance reasons. Using the intelligence built into the new generation of storage hardware to perform these encryption functions can significantly reduce mainframe CPU costs for many clients.

Reducing Total Cost of Ownership

Despite its well-understood scalability and resilience advantages, the System z platform needs to continue to demonstrate that it represents good value for money in today's competitive IT environment. Reducing the total cost of ownership (TCO) for System z applications is therefore an ongoing theme, and DB2 9 introduces a number of important advances in this area.

Clone tables. In today's high-availability environments, some processes can cause an unacceptable amount of disruption to applications needing to access the data. One solution to this problem is to create a copy of the table, keep it in step with the original, and temporarily allow applications to access the table copy when disruptive operations are being run against the original. This process is effective, but it requires a large amount of design and implementation effort on behalf of the application developer and DBA. DB2 9 introduces direct support for "cloned" tables, letting the DBA create an exact copy of a table with a simple command and allowing application access to be easily switched between the original and the clone.

Optimization Service Center. Business pressures often lead to applications being written and implemented very quickly, with little time available for performance testing and tuning. The Optimization Service Center (OSC) is a no-charge GUI workstation tool that is offered as part of the optional DB2 Accessories Suite for z/OS. It provides a host of facilities DBAs can use to identify and analyze problem SQL statements and perform various tuning tasks.

Universal table spaces. The "partition-by-growth" feature described earlier lets DB2 manage disk space growth for some tables, removing the requirement for DBAs to closely monitor and manage it themselves.

Automatic object creation. Unlike many other database implementations, prior versions of DB2 for z/OS used to insist on the DBA explicitly creating all the prerequisite DB2 objects (e.g., databases as table spaces) before a table could be created. DB2 9 improves compatibility with other database systems and reduces DBA workload by allowing these objects to be automatically created by DB2.

Database roles. This new feature permits a predefined set of DB2 authorities to be easily allocated to individuals and removed when no longer required, with associated savings in security administration effort.

Dynamic schema change. DB2 V8 introduced some major enhancements to allow database structures to be altered dynamically. This capability significantly improves data availability but also improves DBA productivity as complex scripts to drop and re-create database objects can be replaced by a single command. DB2 9 further enhances these abilities by allowing yet more changes to be made online.

Recover to consistent point. DBA productivity is a critical factor during application or DB2 system recovery, where every minute taken to recover can translate directly into lost revenue. One of the most time-consuming tasks during the recovery process is identifying a "consistent point" to recover to—a moment in time when no updates were pending. DB2 9 includes some enhancements to the recover utility to enable DB2 to automatically select a consistent recovery point when the DBA requests a data recovery. This speeds up the recovery process and makes it less prone to error.

SQL merge. A common requirement when updating a database is to perform a merge operation, where source data is used to either update an existing record in the database if it already exists or insert a new record if it does not (this operation is also known as an "upsert"—a combination of update and insert).The new **MERGE** SQL statement introduced in DB2 9 performs this process entirely within DB2, improving developer productivity and enhancing the performance of the application.

Truncate table. Under some circumstances, it is necessary for an administrator to clear down a DB2 table and remove all data from it. A new **TRUNCATE TABLE** command in DB2 9 lets this be done more efficiently than before.

SQL procedures. DB2 9 enhancements to SQL procedures make it feasible for many more clients to begin writing their stored procedures in this language. Because SQL procedures do not need any form of program preparation, they are quicker to prepare and prototype than those written in conventional languages.

Index on expression. The ability to create an index on an SQL expression has the potential to transform the performance of many queries and is expected to be one of the most valuable performance enhancements in DB2 9.

Large object enhancements. The use of LOBs within DB2 for z/OS is increasing rapidly, and a significant amount of effort has been expended by IBM to improve the performance of queries accessing LOBs in DB2 9. The way in which LOBs are locked to enforce consistency has been completely overhauled, and some other enhancements have been implemented to make the handling of large LOBs much more efficient.

Optimization enhancements. The optimizer enhancements previously described will result in significant performance benefits for other types of applications, too.

INSERT *enhancements.* Many applications need to be able to insert large volumes of data into DB2 tables in a limited amount of time. DB2 9 makes several enhancements to DB2 index structures and insert processing to speed up mass insert operations. Initial IBM testing has shown CPU reductions of up to 20 percent as a result of these changes.

Utility enhancements. Utilities are a mundane but vital part of DB2, enabling the DBA to back up, restore, reorganize, and maintain critical business data. IBM has enhanced most of these utilities in DB2 9, with CPU reduction of between 10 and 70 percent being measured internally by IBM.

Sort enhancements. Several improvements have been made to various sorting operations in DB2 9. Depending upon the workload, these have reduced CPU by up to 50 percent for some IBM test queries.

Reordered row format. The reordered row format can yield significant performance benefits when performing large queries against tables with varying-length columns. Although this feature is of limited value for most typical online applications, some heavier queries have shown a performance boost of up to 50 percent as a result of this feature.

Migration APARs for DB2 10

II14477: DB2 9 Migration/Fallback INFOAPAR to/from DB2 10

http://www.ibm.com/support/docview.wss?uid=isg1II14477&myns=swgimgmt&mynp=
   OCSSEPEK&mync=E

II14474: DB2 V8 Migration/Fallback INFOAPAR to/from DB2 10

http://www.ibm.com/support/docview.wss?uid=isg1II14474&myns=swgimgmt&mynp=
   OCSSEPEK&mync=E

Notes

1. For more details about IBM's Smarter Planet initiative, see *http://www.ibm.com/ smarterplanet*.

2. For a summary of the DB2 9 business benefits, see the Appendix.

3. To benefit from improvements in DB2's ability to select the most efficient access path, a "rebind" will usually be required to allow DB2 to re-create the access path structures for an application. This does not require any changes to the application.

4. Optimized functions include **IF** and **SET** statement processing and access to the **SYSDUMMY1** table. Exploiting these enhancements requires the stored procedures to be regenerated (or dropped and re-created) but no application change.

5. When upgrading to DB2 10, IBM supports customers moving either from DB2 9 or DB2 V8 via a "skip migration" process. See the "Upgrading to DB2 10" section for further details.

6. An "active thread" is a connection to DB2 that is actively working on behalf of an application requestor. The maximum number of threads supported by a single DB2 system depends on the nature of the workload.

7. Data sharing is an optional DB2 facility that lets multiple DB2 systems (known as "members") access a single shared copy of the data. It is usually implemented to improve availability, as the loss of any single DB2 system allows processing to continue on the others.

8. Traditional DB2 applications usually use "static SQL," which is hard-coded into the application and can therefore be checked and analyzed when the program is prepared, saving valuable elapsed and CPU time when the program is run. Dynamic SQL is not hard-coded and therefore cannot be prepared for execution in advance. It is more flexible than static SQL but often costs more to execute because checking and access path selection can be done only at run time.

9. If a row cannot fit on the correct page due to space limitations, it may be relocated in an overflow area, and therefore two page accesses may sometimes be required. This should not normally occur if the volumes are specified correctly when the table is defined.

10. Parameter markers let literals in SQL statements be replaced with a "?" to represent a host variable in the application.

11. For more details about this feature, see the Appendix.

12. One of the ways in which IBM is reducing the overall cost of mainframe workloads is to offer customers the option of installing additional "specialty processors" within their System z machines. These processors are capable of running only specific types of work, but in so doing they can reduce the load on the general-purpose CP processors and therefore the amount of chargeable CPU consumed. The zIIP is a specialty processor designed to offload specific types of data- and transaction-processing workloads, such as remote SQL statements, some DB2 utility processing, and network encryption.

13. For more details about this feature, see the Appendix.

14. Note that DB2 has long supported backout during system recoveries or system restarts. DB2 10 provides this option for individual table space recoveries for the first time.

15. FlashCopy is a function provided by IBM disk storage systems that allows near-instantaneous copies to be made of data. Other vendors provide similar functionality.

16. This functionality is also available to be retrofitted to DB2 V8 and DB2 9, via APAR PM12256.

17. Via APAR PK52523. For more details, see *http://publib.boulder.ibm.com/infocenter/ dzichelp/v2r2/topic/com.ibm.db29.doc.perf/db2z_usepackagecopy2alleviateperfregress.htm.*

18. Such as **SYSADM** and **DBADM**.

19. Technically, this discussion applies to both the DB2 Catalog and the Directory (which contains internal representations of the objects in the Catalog). The term "Catalog" is used to represent both objects for brevity.

20. APARs are also available for Versions 8 and 9 to provide EAV support.

21. UTC, or Coordinated Universal Time. This is equivalent to GMT (Greenwich Mean Time) and provides a point of reference from which the time zone offsets for locations around the world can be expressed.

22. For further details about the Smart Analytics Optimizer, see the IBM Redbook *Using IBM System z As the Foundation for Your Information Management Architecture*, REDP-4606 (IBM International Technical Support Organization. s.l.: IBM ITSO, 2010).

23. Note that DB2 9 is also supported, with the necessary maintenance applied.

24. In the initial release, there are some restrictions on the type of queries eligible for offload to the Smart Analytics Optimizer blade. These include support for dynamic SQL only (no static SQL), SQL syntax and data type restrictions, and a requirement for tables to be defined in advance to the SAO environment. Some or all of these may be lifted in a future release.

25. TPC-H is a standard ad hoc, decision-support benchmark. For further details, see *http://www. tpc.org/tpch.*

26. Single Version Charging (SVC) lets a customer pay for only the most current version of a program while running both the current and previous versions on the same CPU. This allows a customer a fixed period to upgrade from the previous version to the current version of the program while paying only for the newer version.

27. Stuhler, Julian. *DB2 9 for z/OS – Data on Demand*. White Paper. s.l.: Triton Consulting, 2007.

DB2 10 for z/OS: CPU Savings . . . Right Out of the Box

by Dave Beulke

Executive Summary

DB2 10 for z/OS is a tremendous step forward in database technology because of its improvements in performance, scalability, availability, security, and application integration. Its technology provides a clear competitive advantage through its continued improvements in SQL, XML, and integrated business intelligence capabilities.

DB2 10 leverages the recent advances in chip technology, storage devices, and memory capacities through its extensive exploitation of System z 64-bit architecture to reduce CPU requirements, improve performance, and potentially dramatically reduce the total cost of ownership. DB2 10's CPU reduction features are welcomed around the world as companies analyze every factor to improve the bottom line.

Early adopters and beta customer testing of DB2 10 shows its many enhancements optimize their run-time environments by reducing CPU consumption out-of-the-box by up to 5 to 10 percent. An additional CPU savings of up to 10 percent is also being experienced by companies' systems that specifically leverage DB2 10's many processing and utility improvements. In addition, DB2 10 handles five to 10 times more concurrent users—up to 20,000—providing significant improvements in capacity, scalability, and overall performance for any type of large-scale application.

Capacity, scalability, and performance continue to be DB2 for z/OS's strengths. Through full exploitation of the System z 64-bit architecture, DB2 enhancements such as shorter optimized processing, leveraging of solid-state disk, in-memory workfile enhancements, index insert parallelism improvements, and better SQL/XML access paths provide many reductions in CPU costs and performance improvements without requiring any application changes.

DB2 10 features also enhance continuous business processing, database availability, and overall ease of use. DB2 is continuously available due to more options with online database changes, more concurrent utilities, and easier administration processes. DB2 10 database systems are always available; even while database changes are being done, transactions can be processed. These new database change capabilities, combined with more options for parallel utility execution, provide smaller concurrent windows for processing and administration tasks to streamline your overall system operations.

Security, regulatory compliance, and audit capability improvements are also included in DB2 10. DB2 10's enhanced security extends the role-based model introduced in DB2 9. DB2 10 provides more granular authorities that separate data access from the administration of the application, database, and system. DB2 10 provides administration flexibility for specific security role settings, preventing data access exposure to unauthorized applications or administrators. This role-based security model, combined with the label-based row and column access control and masking or encryption of sensitive information, enhances the ultimate secure database environment for your business. All of these features provide tighter controls, allow more security flexibility, and provide tremendous regulatory and audit compliance capabilities.

Application integration and portability benefit tremendously from the DB2 10 SQL and XML enhancements. DB2 10 SQL improvements further embrace the DB2 family with more enhancements for porting other DBMS vendor products into the DB2 10 for z/OS environment. Additional enhancements with timestamps with time zones, Java timestamp compatibility, and timestamp 12-digit picosecond precision granularity provide unique business transaction timestamps for every transaction in a table. This helps global companies understand all their businesses across all the global events of the day.

Data versioning with current and history tables is also available with DB2 10. Data versioning provides flexibility to migrate current operational data into a historical data table based on set time periods. This enhances the performance for the application operations and maintains your historical data for audit and better integration into your regulatory compliance architecture.

Also, data warehouse and business intelligence capabilities are now built directly into DB2 10 with the new temporal table capabilities and the SQL capabilities for calculating moving sums and moving averages. This enhances your bottom line by integrating business intelligence capabilities into your front-line operational applications.

DB2 10 XML improvements help application flexibility, usability, and performance. Through the ability to replace, delete, or insert XML document nodes, manage multiple XML schema version documents, and utilize the binary pre-tokenized XML format, DB2 10 provides a number of important XML performance and management improvements. Additional enhancements within utilities, date/time data types, and XML parameter support within SQL functions and procedures provide application flexibility to utilize XML within any application architecture solution.

DB2 10 for z/OS delivers performance, scalability, availability, and security while improving application integration and regulatory compliance. By reducing costs and providing superior technology, IBM's DB2 10 remains the technology leader and best-choice database for today's and tomorrow's business systems that seek a competitive advantage.

Section I

Performance Availability

For relational database customers, database performance is paramount. DB2 10 for z/OS has raised the bar by reducing CPU demand by up to 5 to 10 percent immediately out of the box with no application changes. CPU demand can be reduced up to 20 percent once all the DB2 10 enhancements are leveraged in new function mode (NFM). By pushing the performance limits, IBM and DB2 10 continue to lead the database industry with the state-of-the-art technology and the most efficient database processing available.

IBM DB2 10 for z/OS, with its out-of-the-box CPU reduction for applications and many NFM enhancements, delivers the best performance improvements since DB2 Version 2.1. DB2 10 emphasis on performance is pervasive throughout the features and enhancements. Availability, scalability, security, compliance, application integration, XML, and SQL all contain performance improvements. All of these enhancements together provide an improved operational environment, making administration easier while reducing the total cost of ownership for the business.

Many Performance Enhancements

Performance is the major emphasis of DB2 10. Many enhancements make direct reduction in CPU time for applications. By migrating to the new version and deploying and rebinding your applications within the environment, you can leverage many of the performance enhancements in your applications without changing the applications. DB2 10 leverages the full 64-bit architecture, new access paths, and optimization of other access paths and provides performance improvements right out of the box.

Rebinding your applications is now even easier. Concerns about regression are easily addressed with Plan Stability, introduced in DB2 9 and further enhanced in DB2 10. DB2 10 Plan Stability provides administrators the ability to rebind without risking performance. Plan Stability improvements provide parallelism to be turned on for individual packages, giving administrators more options and better control. These new DB2 10 Plan Stability features provide additional flexibility for fine-tuning your application performance and reducing CPU consumption without application changes.

New Optimizer Access Path Range-List Index Scan

DB2 10 offers a new application access path called Range-List Index Scan. This access path improves SQL processing against an index when multiple **WHERE** clauses can all reference the same index. For example, when the SQL has multiple **OR, IN**, or other predicates that reference the same index, the optimizer now recognizes it and scans the index only once instead of multiple times for each of the **WHERE** clause predicates. This immediately cuts down the number of record ID (RID) list entries for the processing, improving I/O and CPU performance.

This new access path can be utilized when all the SQL **WHERE** clauses with multiple **OR** statements reference the same table, at least one of them has a matching predicate, and all would reference the same index. This type of SQL **WHERE** clause with multiple **OR** statements is typical for many types of applications, especially searching, scrolling, or pagination application processes.

Optimizer Uses More Parallelism

DB2 10 also improves several existing access paths through parallelism. These specifically designed enhancements eliminate some previous DB2 restrictions, increase the amount of work redirected to the zIIP processors, and distribute work more evenly across the parallel tasks. All of these enhancements give additional reasons to enable parallelism within your environment.

Parallelism improves your application performance, and DB2 10 can now take full advantage of parallelism with several types of SQL queries, such as multi-row fetch, full outer joins, common table expression (CTE) references, table expression materialization, a table function, a **CREATE GLOBAL TEMPORARY** table (CGTT), or a work file resulting from view materialization. These new DB2 10 CP parallelism enhancements are active when the SQL Explain parallel mode column contains a "C."

The new parallelism enhancements can also be active during several other specialized SQL situations. These situations are:

- When the optimizer chooses index reverse scan for a table
- When an SQL subquery is transformed into join
- When DB2 chooses to do a multiple-column hybrid join with sort composite

- When the leading table is sort output and the join between the leading table and the second table is a multiple-column hybrid join

Additional DB2 10 optimization and access improvements also help many aspects of application performance. In DB2 10, index lookaside and sequential detection help improve referencing parent keys within referential integrity (RI) structures during **INSERT** processing. This is more efficient for checking RI-dependent data and reduces the overall CPU required for the insert activity.

List Prefetch Improves Index Access

List prefetch is utilized more within DB2 10 to access index leaf and non-leaf pages. In previous versions of DB2, when the index became disorganized and had large gaps between non-leaf pages, accessing index entries through sequential reading of non-leaf pages became degraded by huge numbers of synchronous I/Os. DB2 10 improvements use non-leaf page information to perform a list prefetch of the leaf pages. This eliminates most of the synchronous I/Os and the I/O waits associated with the large gaps in the non-leaf pages during the sequential read. This list prefetch processing especially helps long-running queries dependent on non-leaf page access, and it also helps all the index-related utilities, such as **REORG INDEX**, **CHECK INDEX**, and **RUNSTATS**.

Optimizer No Longer Changes Access Path Due to RID Pool Overflows

DB2 10 also improves the handling of SQL statements that reference a large amount of data through list processing. This list processing uses a large number of record IDs and sometimes overflows the RID pool. In previous versions of DB2, the RID pool overflow caused DB2 to change the SQL access method to a table space scan. Now when the RID pool resources are exhausted, the RID list is written to workfile resources and processing continues. This improvement helps avoid the table space scan with its associated elapsed time, locking impact, and performance overhead.

Optimizer Does More During Stage 1 SQL Evaluation

The DB2 10 optimizer can now evaluate scalar functions and non-matching index predicates during the first (Stage 1) evaluation of the SQL access path. The optimizer can apply these previously Stage 2 scalar functions and non-matching predicates early in the optimization process to limit the number of qualifying data pages and rows. This eliminates or reduces the amount of data evaluated in Stage 2, dramatically improving query elapsed time and overall query performance.

Optimizer Determines Which Access Is More Certain

In previous versions of DB2, the optimizer evaluates the SQL **WHERE** predicate, the table indexes available, and various statistics to determine the most efficient access path. With the enhancements in DB2 10, the optimizer analyzes additional filter factor variables, evaluating the SQL range predicate, the non-uniform distribution of the data, and the usage of parameter markers, host variables, or literals where values are unknown.

When choosing between two different indexes, these unknown filter factor variables make the cost estimate between two different access paths very close. Analyzing which of the different filter factor variables are known, DB2 determines which of the index access paths has a higher degree of certainty. DB2 may choose an index access with a slightly higher cost that will provide a more certain run-time performance. This is especially important to provide the best consistent and reliable performance with the different types of programming languages and the application diversity of the parameter markers, literals, and host variables available.

Dynamic Statement Cache ATTRIBUTES Improvements

One of the most important DB2 10 system improvements is the ability to combine some variations of SQL within the dynamic statement cache. Using the new **ATTRIBUTES** clause within the **PREPARE** SQL statement, DB2 is now able to recognize that the SQL is the same except for the **WHERE** clause literal values. This helps DB2 recognize that these statements already exist within the cache and reuse the cache resources previously generated for the SQL statement, helping avoid additional DB2 catalog activity such as object verification and access path creation for another SQL statement. This also helps free more cache space for other SQL statements for reuse, improving performance and transaction response time.

Improved DDF Transaction Flow

Application performance and network transaction traffic are optimized when **SELECT** statements are coded using the **FETCH 1 ROW ONLY** clause. DB2 now recognizes this **SELECT** statement **FETCH 1 ROW ONLY** clause and combines the **OPEN** cursor, **SQL FETCH**, and **CLOSE** cursor into a single request instead of three separate messages flowing across the network through the system.

The change to the **FETCH 1 ROW ONLY** clause also improves the performance of the JDBC and CLI APIs. After the query data is retrieved, the **FETCH 1 ROW ONLY** clause causes the API's default action for DB2 to close the resources. DB2 closes the resources regardless of whether a **CURSOR WITH HOLD** was declared and notifies the API driver to cancel any additional **FETCH** or **CLOSE** statement requests. This dramatically reduces the number and amount of transaction network messages transmitted while improving DB2 performance and minimizing locking contention.

Workfile Enhancements

Several types of SQL statement functionality, such as joins, **GROUP BY**, and **ORDER BY**, utilize workfiles to get their results. DB2 10 can now evaluate simple query predicates against these workfiles, improving overall performance and reducing elapsed time.

Also in the **WORKFILE** database, DB2 10 supports the definition of partition-by-growth (PBG) table spaces to support in-memory tables for improved performance. This provides a dedicated definition type for in-memory data and relieves the extra administration work of defining a single table space within dedicated buffer pools.

In addition, DB2 10 expands the record length size for workfiles to 65,529 bytes for handling larger record size answer sets. This is especially important for handling XML, larger record sorts, and joins.

MEMBER CLUSTER Option

DB2 tries to maintain the table space clustering sequence when data is inserted into the table. For data-sharing systems with robust **INSERT** processing, maintaining the clustering sequence can cause locking contention within the table space across the different data-sharing members. This contention causes extra CPU cycles to negotiate deadlocks and extended response time to maintain the clustering sequence.

DB2 10 partition-by-growth and partition-by-range (PBR) table spaces have a new **MEMBER CLUSTER** parameter that allows DB2 to insert data into the first available space and disregard the clustering sequence of the table space. While this relieves the contention, the clustering sequence of the table space should be monitored. Poor cluster ratios can negatively impact access paths and sometimes cause additional random I/O for critical high-performance applications.

Universal Range-Partitioned Table Space
DB2 10 also continues to enhance the universal range-partitioned table space. This table space is the updated version of the classic range-partitioned table space with additional segment size specification, universal settings, and capabilities. This universal range-partitioned table space is the migration target for the classic range-partitioned table space that is deprecated and may be supported for only a few more DB2 releases.

Database administrators are being encouraged to use the new universal range-partitioned table space instead of the classic range-partition definitions to leverage all the new utility capabilities, availability, and performance features.

Buffer Pool Enhancements
System z handles memory allocations better, and DB2 10 leverages this capability through its buffer pool management enhancements. In previous versions, DB2 allocated the defined size of the buffer pool at startup for use by all the associated table and index objects. In DB2 10, the system allocates the memory for the buffer pools as the data is brought into the buffer pool. This keeps the buffer pool size down to a minimum and to only what is being used by applications.

In addition, DB2 10 reduces its latch contention and provides the ability to define larger buffer pools from current megabytes to gigabytes of memory for your critical active objects. This will definitely improve the system I/O rates and reduce contention.

The new System z10 one-megabyte page size handles larger buffer pools better. Because buffer pool memory allocations can quickly become very large, prudent definitions management and the z10 one-megabyte page size will keep your overall system paging to a minimum and reduce CPU time.

New and Improved Online Schema Changes
Some of the best new features within DB2 10 are the new online schema change features. First, the list of attributes able to be **ALTER**ed on any DB2 table space, index, or table component continues to grow. Within DB2 10, the

list has been further enhanced to take care of the most common activities in an online **ALTER** and then reorg process. Being able to change almost any component of the common database attributes online provides administration flexibility and application availability for almost any changes to your database systems.

A new long list of table space, table, index, and column attributes may now be **ALTER**ed in DB2 10. Some of the new attributes that can be **ALTER**ed are data set size, table/index page size, segment size, and the ability to migrate old-style table space definitions to the new partition-by-growth or partition-by-range universal table spaces.

In addition, DB2 10 online schema enhancements improve adoption of the new attributes by replacing the old operation processes of **DROP/RECREATE** table space/table and **REBUILD** indexes process to only an **ALTER** and then online **REORG** process. When utilizing online **REORG**s, the new **ALTER** and **REORG** process leaves the database tables available for application activity while the new attribute changes are applied into the system. This new method of enhancing the database eliminates down time and provides great relief for mission-critical very large database (VLDB) availability issues.

As DB2 databases continue to grow in size and transaction volume, the amount of administration time required for database changes continues to be a challenge. A number of DB2 utility improvements further minimize downtime during normal operational and database-change activities.

Now also within DB2 10, DBAs will be able to create or rebuild a non-unique index against tables with LOBs without any application impact or locking downtime. This online schema change enhancement will especially help newly installed applications where another index can be quickly defined and dramatically improve SQL access or resolve a performance issue. This enhancement alone can help improve performance instantaneously for any installed application.

The new **ALTER** and **REORG** method of applying changes introduces a new database exception state of **AREOR** to signify that attribute changes are pending. This new database **AREOR** state, along with DB2 catalog tables, utility enhancements, and the **DROP PENDING CHANGES** command, provides full functionality for managing your **ALTER** and **REORG** processes.

INCLUDE Non-Unique Columns Within a Unique Index

One of the schema changes that your applications need right away is the ability to include more columns into unique indexes. This new DB2 10 feature lets non-unique columns be included in the definition of a unique index definition. Before this enhancement, multiple indexes were required for indexing, one for the unique constraint and another index for the non-unique columns. Using the new **CREATE** or **ALTER INCLUDE** clause, a unique index definition can include additional non-unique columns into the definition of the index. This eliminates all the extra I/O spent maintaining the other index along with the additional storage needed for multiple index definitions with similar columns, and it improves performance for all access to the table.

By combining two indexes into a single index definition using the new **INCLUDE** non-unique columns, the new range-list index scan access path can be used because the single index criteria is now satisfied. DB2 can reference the new single index definition with **INCLUDE**d non-unique columns and can potentially improve your application performance by referencing the single index only once and using the new, more efficient access path.

New Hash Space and Access Method

DB2 10 also introduces a completely new access type called Hash Access. A new Hash space supports this new access method. DB2 uses an internal hash algorithm with the Hash space to reference the location of the data rows. In some cases, this direct Hash Access reduces data access to a single I/O, dramatically decreasing the CPU workload and speeding up application response time. Queries that use full key equal predicates, such as customer number or product number lookups, are good candidates for Hash Access. Additional indexes can be created to support other range, list, or keyed access types.

The definition of the Hash space requires a column or columns for the direct Hash Access keys. Each table with Hash Access has an associated Hash space or Hash space partitions. Hash Access requires some additional storage space for dramatically reducing access CPU workload.

Another advantage of Hash Access is no need to maintain a clustering index or data sequence. This allows for efficient insert processing and avoids data sharing contention for maintaining a clustering sequence or clustering index.

There are tradeoffs for using Hash Access. Parallelism is not available and traditional clustering is not allowed for the hash data. Nevertheless, Hash Access will be beneficial for database designs where unique keys are already using equal predicates on product or customer IDs, object IDs, XML document IDs, and other direct key retrievals.

DB2 Catalog Enhancements

The DB2 10 catalog and directory are restructured, removing special structures and links. Through this restructuring, the DB2 catalog now uses the new universal partition-by-growth table spaces, reordered row format, and one table per table space, thus expanding the number of DB2 catalog table spaces. These new universal table spaces are defined with **DSSIZE 64 MAXPART 1**, row-level locking, and some CLOB and BLOB data types to handle repeating long strings. These common table space definitions allow the catalog tables to be managed like your application database with online reorganizations and check utilities.

In addition to these enhancements, the **UTSERIAL** lock that caused lock contention with older versions of DB2 utility processing has been eliminated. This improvement, along with a reduction in log latch contention through a new compare and swap logic, the new option of readers to avoid waiting for inserters, and improvements in system thread latching serialization, helps reduce many types of DB2 thread-processing contention. All these enhancements help tremendously with concurrency of DDL, **BIND**, utility, and overall processing within your application database systems and especially in processes referencing the DB2 catalog.

Another enhancement provides the ability to add a new log into the system inventory while the subsystem is active. The newly added log is immediately available without recycling DB2, which should help recovery procedures and application performance.

Section II

Scalability, Simplification, Security

Improvements in several key areas of database technology make DB2 10 for z/OS more scalable, usable, and secure than ever.

Full 64-bit Runtime Environment Exploited

DB2 10 dramatically improves scalability with more exploitation of the 64-bit System z environment. Exploiting the 64-bit environment and moving 80 to 90 percent of the DB2 memory that is now below the bar—working storage, EDMPOOL, and even some ECSA—above the 2GB bar eliminates the main memory constraints within the DB2 **DBM1** address space for most systems.

Large Increase in the Number of Users (Up to 20,000)

By addressing this memory constraint in the overall system, virtual memory monitoring is no longer necessary, as five to 10 times more concurrent threads can be run in a single DB2 10 member. The increase in threads removes one key reason for additional DB2 data sharing members and allows some consolidation of LPARs and members previously built for handling more end users. This enables more available memory on constrained machines where multiple data sharing members were taking real storage, causing additional maintenance and operational overhead.

Parallel Inserts into Multiple Indexes

DB2 10 also improves insert performance by using more parallelism. When **INSERT SQL** modifies a table with multiple indexes, DB2 10 does the prefetch of multiple indexes in parallel. By initiating parallel I/Os for the multiple indexes, the process is not waiting for the synchronous I/Os, reducing the overall insert process time. This cuts down the time frame of possible contention within your system and improves performance of all your applications.

Plan Stability: Package Preservation

The Plan Stability features in DB2 9 offer an enhanced way to handle testing of a new version of a DB2 application package. Plan Stability offers a way to save DB2 access packages for an application and then **REBIND** a new one. If the access package is not as efficient, Plan Stability gives the administrator the ability to switch back to the previous version of the package with a simple **REBIND SWITCH** to the old version of the package.

DB2 10 expands on this functionality by providing the capability to handle many versions of DB2 packages. Plan stability has the ability to allow management of two or three copies of old static SQL packages controlled through the DB2 **PLANMGMT** parameter and **REBIND** parameters.

Through the **REBIND SWITCH** parameter, administrators can pick whatever version of the package they want. This gives the application team the flexibility to evaluate performance and to get the best-performing version of the package implemented. This DB2 10 enhancement removes the trepidation of rebinding an application and helps administrators protect their critical applications' performance.

RUNSTATS Improvements and Auto Stats

Because the optimizer access paths improve performance dramatically, up-to-the-moment statistics are vital. DB2 10 comes with a new set of stored procedures to monitor and collect table and index statistics. These new procedures monitor the current statistics, determine whether new statistics need to be collected, and then autonomically perform the collection to ensure good access path optimization.

These procedures especially help volatile environments and can dynamically help improve access path optimization by getting index filtering statistics for SQL **WHERE** clause predicates to make the best access path decisions. By gathering statistics for you, these DB2 10 stored procedures take the burden off administrators for large and especially dynamically created objects to help ensure overall application performance.

Improved and Finer-Grained Access Control

DB2 10 also includes security, regulatory compliance, and audit capabilities improvements. DB2 10 enhances the DB2 9 role-based security with additional administrative and other finer-grained authorities and privileges. This authority granularity helps separate administration and data access, providing only the minimum appropriate authority.

The new **SECADM** authorization level provides the authority to manage access to the tables while prohibiting creating, dropping, or altering any access to the tables. The enhanced **DBADM** authority provides an option to have administration capabilities without data access. These authority profiles provide better separation of duties while limiting blanket authority over all aspects of a table and its data.

In addition, DB2 10 embraces audit and regulatory compliance through a new audit policy that provides a set of criteria for auditing for the possible abuse and overlapping of authorities within a system. This helps management, administrators, and the business community understand, configure, and audit security policies and data access quickly for any role or user. Many audit policies can be developed to quickly verify audit and document the security compliance across your environment's critical data resources and their application users.

Support for Row and Column Access Control

DB2 10 also enhances security through its row and column access control. This access control lets administrators enable security on a particular column or a particular row in the database. This security limits the data seen by any end user by not allowing that column or row to be returned in the answer to a user's query unless the user has the proper authority based on his or her security level. This capability permits very fine-grained security to be defined against any data. The role-based security model, combined with the label-based row and column access control and masking or encryption of sensitive information, enhances the ultimate secure database environment for your business. All of these features provide tighter controls, allow more security flexibility, and provide tremendous regulatory and audit compliance capabilities.

Section III

Application Enablement

Applications benefit in numerous ways from DB2 10's XML support, new temporal data functionality, data type enhancements, and improved SQL compatibility.

pureXML Enhancements

Within DB2 10, XML can be used almost anywhere within SQL variables, scalar functions, SQL table functions, and SQL procedures. DB2 10 pureXML incorporates many new enhancements that improve overall XML performance, provide easier XML schema management, and embrace DB2 family compatibility.

These enhancements start with XML schema validation that is now built into DB2 10. The XML schema no longer needs to be specified because DB2 handles XML schema validation more easily through a built-in function that validates the XML schemas. DB2 uses the timestamp to match up the XML document to the correct schema version. This allows multiple schema versions to coexist and validate new or older XML documents against their appropriate XML schema versions.

Additional functionality enhancements provide the capability to manipulate any part of an XML document. By using SQL statements with XML expressions, any single or multiple XML document nodes can be inserted, updated, or deleted or have their data values updated. This provides tremendous XML document capabilities, overall performance, and flexibility for any application process.

DB2 10 also provides a new XML type modifier that enforces and validates the XML document column data against the schema definition information. This new modifier is used when adding or removing XML schemas and can be **ALTER**ed onto older XML schemas so their XML column types can be validated. This helps ensure that the XML schema documents' stored elements have only the desired XML content.

Support for XML Date and Time

DB2 10 also has expanded date and timestamp options with time zone XML data types. These data types are supported within XML indexes, and the timestamp is expanded to handle more precision for finer data management. DB2 10 also comes with new XML time and date arithmetic comparison functions to further support application processing.

Binary XML Support

DB2 10 improves XML with new support for binary XML objects. Binary support is important because binary format is better for server and application interaction. Binary support uses pre-tokenized format and length definitions, which improve overall performance of binary XML objects and provide additional ease of use for application definitions.

Binary XML also has additional flexibility features such as String IDs for text that represents some or all occurrences of the same text with an integer identifier. This feature can help limit the size of XML. Working with the same text improves application performance.

Faster Streaming of XML and LOBs

DB2 10 provides a new **LOB_INLINE_LENGTH** installation parameter that sets the default number of bytes for storing inline LOBs. Having a minimized LOB length or a predefined standard length provides better streaming capabilities and the ability to minimize and optimize the use of the inline LOB space.

Minimizing the LOB size or eliminating LOB or XML materialization reduces the memory consumption and improves CPU for LOB operations. This is especially beneficial during LOB **LOAD** utilities that use a file reference variable for the LOB data, inserting LOB or XML data from remote DRDA server applications, and when inserting a single LOB or XML value into a row. Using the new **LOB_INLINE_LENGTH** options in all of these cases minimizes the number of bytes required and streamlines XML and LOB operations.

XML Define (NO) for LOB and XML TS

Administrators now have the option to delay the definition of the LOB or XML data sets and their indexes. This helps save storage space by defining them into the DB2 Catalog and letting the application **SELECT** and **FETCH** them. The LOB or XML data sets and their indexes are allocated only when the first insert is done, conserving storage and application performance until the data is really saved in the database.

The administrator also can use the **CHECK DATA** utility to check the consistency between the XML schema, its document data, and its XML index data.

Temporal Queries and Their Business Advantages

DB2 10 provides new temporal data functionality by using two new **BUSINESS_ TIME** and **SYSTEM_TIME** table period definitions. These new period definitions are used for new temporal table definitions to provide system-maintained, period-maintained, or bi-temporal (both system- and period-maintained) data stores. These temporal data tables are automatically maintained, and when the designated time-period criterion is met, the data is archived to an associated history table.

The **PERIOD SYSTEM_TIME** or **PERIOD BUSINESS_TIME** definition over two columns defines the temporal period for the data within the table. There are many definition restrictions on these temporal period columns. The **SYSTEM_TIME** relates to the time the data was put into the system. The **BUSINESS_TIME** relates to the business transaction or business-relevant time period of the data. These definitions control the criteria for which data exists in the table and when it is migrated to the associated history table. By using both definitions, **PERIOD SYSTEM_TIME** and **PERIOD BUSINESS_TIME**, a table has bi-temporal criteria that control the data that exists in the table.

With the new **BUSINESS_TIME WITHOUT OVERLAPS** definition parameter, the temporal tables also can make all your transaction timestamps unique. This is done using the new **TIMESTAMP** picosecond precision (precision 12) enhancements to provide unique transaction timestamps across the entire temporal table. This is a great advantage for robust global systems previously having issues with the uniqueness of business timestamp transactions.

When SQL is executed against the temporal table, the key **WHERE** clause predicate **FOR (SYSTEM_TIME or BUSINESS_TIME) FROM columna TO columnb** or other similar predicate can be used in the SQL to get only data that is within your temporal time frame. This both helps and complicates your SQL processing because **INSERT** or **DELETE** statements against temporal tables can result in multiple rows being inserted or modified in the table.

If the period specified by the start value and the end value for the **BUSINESS_ TIME** of a row is only partially contained in the specified SQL **WHERE** predicate for an executed **DELETE** SQL statement, that row is deleted, and then one or two additional rows are inserted. The inserted rows represent the original row values for the periods not deleted by the delete operation. For the newly inserted rows, the start value and end value for the **BUSINESS_TIME** are set in such a way as to reflect data not affected by the **DELETE** SQL statement. Therefore, either the start value for the **BUSINESS_TIME** is the start value for the **BUSINESS_TIME** of the original row and the end value is the beginning predicate value, or the start value is the ending predicate value and the end value is the end value for the **BUSINESS_TIME** of the original row.

The processing for an SQL **UPDATE** against a temporal table has similar considerations because an update can also result in additional rows inserted into the table to handle the **BUSINESS_TIME** configuration.

Example #1: Create a table, **policy_info**, that uses a **SYSTEM_TIME** period, and create a history table, **hist_policy_info**. Then issue an **ALTER TABLE** statement to associate the **policy_info** table with the **hist_policy_info** table (this and the subsequent examples are from the *IBM SQL Reference* manual):

```
CREATE TABLE policy_info
(policy_id CHAR(10) NOT NULL,
coverage INT NOT NULL,
sys_start TIMESTAMP(12) NOT NULL GENERATED ALWAYS AS ROW BEGIN,
sys_end TIMESTAMP(12) NOT NULL GENERATED ALWAYS AS ROW END,
create_id TIMSESTAMP(12) GENERATED ALWAYS AS TRANSACTION START ID,
PERIOD SYSTEM_TIME(sys_start,sys_end));

CREATE TABLE hist_policy_info
(policy_id CHAR(10) NOT NULL,
coverage INT NOT NULL,
sys_start TIMESTAMP(12) NOT NULL,
sys_end TIMESTAMP(12) NOT NULL,
create_id TIMESTAMP(12));

ALTER TABLE policy_info
ADD VERSIONING USE HISTORY TABLE hist_policy_info;
```

Example #2: Create a table, **policy_info**, that uses a **BUSINESS_TIME** period:

```
CREATE TABLE policy_info
(policy_id CHAR(4) NOT NULL,
coverage INT NOT NULL,
bus_start DATE NOT NULL,
bus_end DATE NOT NULL,
PERIOD BUSINESS_TIME(bus_start, bus_end));
```

Example #3: Create a table, **policy_info**, that uses both a **SYSTEM_TIME** period and a **BUSINESS_TIME** period to keep historical rows and track a user-specified time period. A table that specifies both a **SYSTEM_TIME** and a **BUSINESS_TIME** is sometimes referred to as a bi-temporal table. To enable retention of historical rows, a history table, **hist_policy_info**, also needs to be created and associated (using the **ALTER TABLE** statement) with the **policy_info** table:

```
CREATE TABLE policy_info
(policy_id CHAR(4) NOT NULL,
coverage INT NOT NULL,
bus_start DATE NOT NULL,
bus_end DATE NOT NULL,
sys_start TIMESTAMP(12) NOT NULL GENERATED ALWAYS AS ROW BEGIN,
sys_end TIMESTAMP(12) NOT NULL GENERATED ALWAYS AS ROW END,
create_id TIMESTAMP(12) GENERATED ALWAYS AS TRANSACTION START ID,
PERIOD BUSINESS_TIME(bus_start, bus_end),
PERIOD SYSTEM_TIME(sys_start, sys_end));

CREATE TABLE hist_policy_info
(policy_id CHAR(4) NOT NULL,
coverage INT NOT NULL,
bus_start DATE NOT NULL,
bus_end DATE NOT NULL,
sys_start TIMESTAMP(12) NOT NULL,
sys_end TIMESTAMP(12) NOT NULL,
create_id TIMESTAMP(12));

ALTER TABLE policy_info
ADD VERSIONING USE HISTORY TABLE hist_policy_info;
```

Timestamp, TIME ZONE, and Other Data Type Enhancements

DB2 10 enhances the **TIMESTAMP** data type with greater precision and provides a new time-zone–sensitive capability, providing more compatibility and functionality for all types of applications.

The **TIMESTAMP** precision enhancement supports up to 12 digits of fractional seconds (picoseconds), with the default matching the Java default of six digits' precision of fractional seconds. The six digits default also helps Java functionality and DB2 Family compatibility, along with SQL Server compatibility. The enhanced **CURRENT TIMESTAMP** uses a special register so applications can specify the desired fractional precision for their application requirements. The precision of the timestamp seconds can also be adjusted to zero or three digits if that satisfies the application requirements.

The **TIMESTAMP** with **TIMEZONE** is a new DB2 data type. This new data type incorporates the new **TIMESTAMP** 12-digit fractional seconds capabilities and also uses the new industry-standard Universal Coordinated Time (UTC), replacing the old Greenwich Mean Time (GMT). This enhancement gives applications additional **TIMEZONE** capabilities to compare business divisions along the same exact timeline across the world, a capability that is vital for global financial, retail, and banking systems.

Access to Currently Committed Data

With five to 10 times more concurrent threads within a single DB2 member, DB2 10 focuses a significant amount of enhancements on application concurrency. DB2 now provides an individual package option for managing concurrency within your applications. This enhancement provides a DB2 package-level **BIND** parameter to let you choose the way your applications should handle data concurrency situations.

DB2 10 introduces the new **CURRENTACCESSRESOLUTION** parameter with the **USECURRENTLYCOMMITTED** and **WAITFOROUTCOME** settings. These parameter settings override the DB2 subsystem parameters **EVALUNC** and **SKIPUNCI** and help the application package quickly perform the desired concurrency action.

The **USECURRENTLYCOMMITTED** setting instructs the system to ignore rows that are in the process of being inserted and use only currently committed rows. This clause is contingent on the package **BIND** isolation level settings being either Cursor Stability or Read Stability.

The **WAITFOROUTCOME** setting instructs the system to wait for the rows that are in-flight to be resolved through a rollback or commit. This causes the application to wait for insert or delete activities to be committed or rolled back before determining the rows that will be included in the application SQL answer set.

These different settings give the application the flexibility to handle highly concurrent Web transactions, wait, or use uncommitted data and provide tremendous flexibility to the enterprise architecture. The different parameter settings help provide the desired package level of concurrency and also provide capabilities that mimic some other database vendors' application concurrency settings.

SQL Compatibility Improvements

DB2 10 provides a substantial list of enhancements for SQL compatibility, including a new extended indicator variable, extended support for implicit casting, enhanced scalar function support, and SQL procedural language enhancements.

Extended Indicator Variable

DB2 10 introduces a new extended indicator variable that provides a way to specify that there is no value provided for an **INSERT**, **UPDATE**, and **MERGE** statement column. As the extended indicator variable name implies, this enhancement extends the functionality that can be used within an indicator variable for providing values within an SQL statement. For example, a value of **–5** within an enabled extended indicator variable specifies the **DEFAULT** value. If the extended indicator variables are not enabled on the SQL package, the **–5** specifies a **NULL** value.

If the extended indicator value is enabled and given a value of **–7**, this indicates that the variable is to be **UNASSIGNED**, ignored, and treated as if it did not exist within the SQL statement. These extended indicator variables are typically for Java applications and are quite useful for dynamic statements and variable SQL statement coding, where the number of possible host variable parameters is unknown until the transaction logic is completed and the SQL is to be executed.

This feature addresses the application issue that previously required multiple SQL statements coded to match the values that were available for the SQL statements. Now, these multiple SQL statements can be consolidated. When the column value is not known, the host variable value can use the new keyword **UNASSIGNED** for the appropriate column(s).

This capability is especially important for applications using dynamic statements that are clogging up their system's Dynamic Statement Cache with many copies of essentially the same SQL statements.

Extended Support for Implicit Casting

Implicit casting is the automatic conversion of different types of data to be compatible. DB2 enhances its implicit casting by handling numeric data types that are able to be implicitly cast to character or graphical string data types. It also supports converting the data in the other direction, from character or graphical string data types to numeric data types.

In previous releases of DB2, this had to be done manually and was a labor-intensive application process. Now numeric, character, and graphical string data can be handled, compared, and assigned implicitly. DB2 for z/OS is more compatible and enhances portability of SQL from other database vendor systems.

Enhanced Scalar Function Support

DB2 10 enhances its compatibility with other database vendors with improvements in SQL scalar and table functions. These built-in functions are used throughout application SQL, making quick work of OLAP functions and calculations such as **SUM**, **AVG**, **SIN**, **COS**, and many others. As in previous releases, these inline functions with their SQL statements return a single value.

Non-inline SQL scalar functions that contain logic provide additional application functionality and flexibility. This flexibility helps DB2 family compatibility and acceptance of data migrations from other database vendors. DB2 also supports multiple versions and source code management of these functions based on their parameter list, routine options, and function body. These functions can be altered, replaced with different versions, and distributed to multiple servers to assist in testing and overall performance. Function version fallback to a previous version is done instantly without a rebind or recompile when a function version is dropped.

DB2 10 introduces support for SQL user-defined table functions that helps ease application migrations from other database vendors. DB2 table functions are very flexible because they return a single data table result based on the many different type of parameters, such as LOBs, distinct types, and transition tables.

SQL Procedural Language Enhancements

DB2 9 provided new native support for the SQL procedural language, eliminating the cumbersome requirement to generate a C program from the SQL procedure that would then execute as an external stored procedure. DB2 9 SQL procedures can be executed natively within the DB2 engine for better runtime execution and stored in the DB2 catalog for better management and version control. Running the native code within the DB2 engine also helps in debugging, deploying, and managing SQL procedural versions across multiple servers. Storing the SQL procedures improves the overall change control of this application code so that it can be managed like your other application developer modules.

The SQL procedural language has many enhancements, including SQL table functions, nested compound SQL statements within a procedure, and the

RETURN statement that can return the result set of a **SELECT** SQL statement. These stored procedure and the other SQL procedural language enhancements allow all types of processing.

The DB2 10 SQL procedural language enhancements provide needed compatibility with other database vendors. The procedure language enhanced ability to accept many data types and XML as parameters and to provide limited use of scrollable cursors provides great compatibility and integration opportunities for your applications. DB2 10's concurrency improvements, along with its SQL procedural language compatibility, provide the opportunity to migrate other relational database management solutions to the z/OS environment for a better cost-of-ownership experience while providing the unique performance, availability, and scalability capabilities that can be found only with DB2 for z/OS and System z.

Section IV

Data Warehousing

DB2 10 has many features and functions that make it a great platform for data warehousing applications. Enhancements such as the new temporal data enhancements, many automatic SQL optimizer enhancements, the new Hash Access plan, SQL scalar and table functions, new timestamp nanosecond and no overlap precision, timestamp with time-zone support, and all the other performance, availability, and scalability improvements contribute to its superiority for data warehousing and business intelligence applications.

Support for Temporal Tables and Versioning

The temporal data enhancements in DB2 10 are a major advance that can automatically archive and version data into your history tables as the business time and system time change. This automatic archiving, coupled with partition-by-growth table spaces, allows automatic expansion as the data comes into and is then archived in the system.

Many new SQL optimizer enhancements improve performance for many more ad hoc queries submitted through OLAP third-party tools or through ODBC connections from Microsoft Excel spreadsheets, handling many more concurrent users. These ad hoc queries with their business time or system time criteria will properly handle the time aspect of the bi-temporal data warehouse SQL questions and return the users' desired answers.

The new Hash Access plan reduces the retrieval of dimension information down to a single I/O for great response time, while the SQL scalar and table functions aggregate and augment the non-overlapping data into a new Java precision interface within a global time-zone–aware context for enterprise scope analysis. All of these features and capabilities, coupled with the highly available, scalable, and reliable System z platform, offer a data warehouse platform for optimum system performance and operational business intelligence systems delivered to the entire enterprise.

OLAP Functionality Built Directly into DB2

The OLAP capabilities of moving sums, averages, and aggregates are now built into DB2. Improvements within SQL, intermediate workfile results, and scalar or table functions provide performance for these OLAP activities.

Moving sums, averages, and aggregates are common OLAP functions within any data warehousing application. These moving sums, averages, and aggregates are typical standard calculations that are done using different groups of location- or time-period–based data for product sales, store location, or other common criteria. Having these OLAP capabilities built directly into DB2 provides an industry-standard SQL process, repeatable applications, SQL function or table functions, and robust performance through better optimization processes.

These OLAP capabilities are further enhanced through scalar, custom table functions or the new temporal tables to establish the window of data for the moving sum, average, or aggregate to calculate its answer set. By using a partition, time frame, or common table SQL expression, the standard OLAP functions can provide the standard calculations for complex or simple data warehouse requirements. Also, given the improvements within SQL, these moving sums, averages, and aggregates can be included in expressions, select lists, or **ORDER BY** statements, satisfying any application requirements.

Advanced Business Analytics

The standard and customizable capabilities that are now available in DB2 10 provide advanced business analytics and fertile ground for customization. Built-in pureXML, LOB, and open SQL scalar and table function interfaces provide many functions and capabilities that can be extended to any type of custom functionality for business requirements.

Temporal tables and their ability to automatically archive historical data provide active data management to help improve performance, audit, and compliance capabilities. Coupled with SQL that can now use business-time or system-time SQL parameters to qualify the answer, DB2 10 provides unique industry-leading-database advanced business analytical capabilities.

Section V

Reduced Total Cost of Ownership

DB2 10 reduces the total DB2 CPU demand from up to 5 to 20 percent in many different ways when all the new enhancements are fully leveraged. Many CPU reductions are built directly into DB2, requiring no application changes. Some enhancements are implemented through normal everyday DB2 activities through rebinding, restructuring database definitions, improving your applications, and utility processing. All of these CPU demand-reduction features have the potential to provide significant total cost of ownership (TCO) savings based on your shop's application mix and transaction types.

Improvements in optimization reduce costs by processing your SQL automatically with more efficient data access paths. Improvements through a new range-list index scan access method, in-list pre-fetch, more parallelism for select and index insert processing, better workfile usage, better RID pool overflow management, access path certainty evaluation, and improved DDF transaction flow all provide more efficiency without any changes to your applications. All of these enhancements reduce your total CPU enterprise costs because of better efficiency in the new DB2 10 for z/OS.

Other enhancements require new database definitions or application programming techniques to reduce your overall costs. These enhancements, such as the Hash Access space and access method, including columns on a unique index, consolidating SQL by using the new Attributes feature, and automatic data statistics, significantly reduce CPU costs through improved access paths.

Reduced costs also come through better operations and improved availability with DB2 10. Its better memory management, ability to handle five to 10 times more users, ability to skip locked rows, improvements in the DB2 catalog, more online schema change capabilities, and more online utilities all eliminate system downtime costs. DB2 10 keeps the application available even while more users, applications, database changes, and utilities are executing in the system.

More automated processes help install, configure, and simplify the installation of your new DB2 10 system. Pre-migration installation steps capture existing settings and provide appropriate settings for the new DB2-supplied routines and programs. These new procedures are meant to reduce installation, configuration, and testing and reduce your time to value for your DB2 10 system.

The ability to migrate directly from DB2 V8 also allows shops that are behind in their software versions to skip implementing DB2 9. Even though such shops will not be able to leverage every DB2 9 for z/OS performance enhancement, skipping Version 9 relieves the burden of going through the software installation, testing, and implementation of an interim step to DB2 10. Migrating directly from Version 8 to Version 10 also provides a quick way to leverage all the great features within DB2 9 and DB2 10 immediately.

DB2 10 offers tremendous value by reducing operational and maintenance costs while improving performance. Plan to install your version of DB2 10 as soon as possible to take advantage of all these great features.

Useful URLs

DB2 for z/OS Family
http://www-01.ibm.com/software/data/db2/zos/family

DB2 10
http://www.ibm.com/software/data/db2/db210

World of DB2 for z/OS
http://db2forzos.ning.com

DB2 for z/OS LinkedIn Group
http://www.linkedin.com/groups?gid=2821100

DB2 for z/OS Twitter
http://twitter.com/IBMDB2

International DB2 Users Group (IDUG)
http://www.idug.org

IDUG Australasia	*http://www.linkedin.com/e/vgh/2656369*
IDUG EMEA	*http://www.linkedin.com/e/vgh/2648157*
IDUG India	*http://www.linkedin.com/e/vgh/2656395*
IDUG North America	*http://www.linkedin.com/e/vgh/2633325*